The Bahá'í Faith
Dawn of a New Day

The Bahá'í Faith
Dawn of a New Day

JESSYCA RUSSELL GAVER

Hawthorn Books, Inc.
Publishers
New York City

First Edition, January, 1967

ACKNOWLEDGMENTS

The author and publisher herewith render thanks to the Bahá'í Publishing Trust, 110 Linden Avenue, Wilmette, Illinois 60091, whose permission to reprint has made possible the publication of this book.

© 1939 The Advent of Divine Justice
© 1950 Bahá'u'lláh and the New Era
© 1945 Bahá'í Administration
© 1943 Bahá'í World Faith
© 1965 Citadel of Faith
© 1956 The Bahá'í World, Volume XII
The Dawn-Breakers, 1932 edition
© 1955 God Passes By
© 1950 The Martyrdom of the Báb
Paris Talks, London, 1951
The Promulgation of Universal Peace, 1943 edition
Star of the West (Bahá'í Magazine, Volume XI)
© 1930, 1954, 1964 Some Answered Questions

0445

Contents

The Need for a World Religion   7

The Bahá'í Way of Life   19

The Dawn and the New Day   48

The Center of the Covenant—'Abu'l-Bahá   77

The Guardianship of the Faith   104

The International Aspects of the Faith   133

America's Destiny in the Bahá'í World   162

The Path of the True Beliver   182

Summation, Personal Comment, Acknowledgments   211

Index   218

This Bahá'í effort is dedicated with
sincerest love to
two special Bahá'í friends:
MMR—my inspiration
RQ—my teacher
and to my beloved daughter, Claudia

The Need for a

World Religion

EARLY IN 1965, American newspapers wrote that Dr. Edwin T. Dahlberg, a former president of the National Council of Churches, had announced we may be on the brink of a new religious revival.

"What is needed," he said, "is a 'prophet' to confront the world with both a personal and a social gospel. It is not enough to evangelize people as individuals. We must assert the Lordship of Jesus Christ over the whole of life—its culture, its industry, its structure.

"There must be both a personal and a social gospel. If we have an evangelism without a social gospel, we have a religion in an ethical vacuum—a church wrapped up in its prayers, feeling pure and agreeable in the presence of God, but failing to be baptized into a feeling of the conditions of the people.

"If, on the other hand, we have a social gospel without personal evangelism, we are in danger of having only a legislative program with no transforming spiritual power."

He noted that despite reasons for despair in the world today "positive aspects of our generation . . . give hope of a far-reaching revival," and listed three conditions that, historically, have been necessary for religious awakenings.

7

1. "A growing sense of discontent and concern regarding moral trends of the time.

2. "A yearning for something better.

3. "The appearance of a messenger, or prophet, who speaks with a voice of authority and whose accent the people will instinctively recognize and obey."

Dr. Dahlberg concluded: "The first two of these three conditions are already in operation. We have yet to welcome the messenger, who will give voice to the higher conscience of the nation and the world."

There are many people who differed with some of Dr. Dahlberg's remarks, among them members of the Bahá'í Faith, the world's fastest growing and youngest independent religion. The Bahá'ís feel that since 1844 *all,* not merely two, of Dr. Dahlberg's conditions have been met, including the appearance of a Prophet (or Messenger) divinely ordained and inspired, Who has given voice and Whose teachings will continue to give voice to the higher conscience and needs of the world, until the next "Coming."

The name of this Divine Messenger is Bahá'u'lláh (meaning, "The Glory and Splendor of God"). His followers are Bahá'ís ("Followers of the Glory"). With His appearance, there came a new light on earth, a slowly developing awareness that there was a world consisting of many peoples, races, creeds, religions, policies, politics, and truths. Bahá'u'lláh's Plan was to bring a way for the first time for all these divergent areas to blend together in unity and oneness, to recognize that while all people may not feel the same way about all things, they can live together in peace and harmony and love.

Bahá'u'lláh's tenets have now been established in thousands of centers in the United States, and throughout the world, and were created to answer the various needs of this day, just as Christ, Moses, and the other divine prophets brought a solution for their own social order and time. However, the fact that the cure is here for the world's sickness doesn't mean the malady is

dead. To Bahá'ís it means that the upheavals of the world today
are the death pangs of the world's old order making way for the
new.

As long ago as 1948 the late Guardian of the Bahá'í Faith,
Shoghi Effendi Rabbani, pronounced the world "politically con-
vulsed, economically disrupted, socially subverted, morally de-
cadent, and spiritually moribund," and the words are just as true
right now. This was not an arbitrary judgment or an invective,
nor was it a hasty analysis overlooking certain important facts.
The Bahá'í point of view reflects upon the world as a whole, and
relates its own ideas to man's fundamental purpose and responsibility.

The Bahá'ís believe that man everywhere must unite or perish.
Since man is in reality a spiritual being, there can be no reality
without unity on a spiritual level as well as a material one.
Bahá'u'lláh's coming not only validates the prophecies of all the
other divinely revealed religions, but through His teachings there
is now at hand the manner whereby the various people of different faiths can unite under God's Plan for today's needs.

Every time man thinks he is in danger, he tries to flee or hide.
Even though aware of the danger under which the world is today,
that the calamity of war rages incessantly, the Bahá'í view is
that man must not retreat from chaos but must rise above it. The
historical figures of the Bahá'í Faith stood in the forefront of all
the dangers and threats rained down upon them, then went
forth to meet the enemies. They didn't retire behind a mountain
or hide beneath a tree.

The Bahá'ís believe that the only refuge in calamity is trust
in God. Prayer is fine, but in addition to praying one must do
something about peril, especially if it can be done according to
Divine Plan. From year to year the Bahá'ís have been given
bigger and bigger responsibilities as part of their goal in carrying the Message of Bahá'u'lláh around the universe. They hope
to convince all of mankind to face the problems that come
with the spread of a new and different divine teaching, because

security comes from the Will of God, not from the schemes of men.

What are these dangers and calamities? We are sitting on top of a time-bomb, and to the Bahá'ís there can be no answer without turning to God. Look at the chaos around us, they suggest, at the many "cold" wars in which even America has already become embroiled. Look at the many nations attacking each other for varying reasons, the attempts to get men of good will to take sides, regardless of whether the motive is pure or evil.

Because Bahá'ís have no prejudices, they have no problems of assimilation wherever they go. Because they believe in having neither too much nor too little material wealth, they are satisfied to have just enough, and gladly sacrifice luxuries in their endeavors to help others. And because they are practical, despite having a spiritual solution, they accept that education is only part of the answer, since education has given us science and science has helped create the weapons of war and destruction. Such weapons include the fiendishly clever crematoriums which made Hitler an object of disgust and despair even to his own countrymen.

The Bahá'ís realize that the world periodically becomes overcrowded, and that countries and peoples try reaching out—for more food, for more space, even for more air to breathe. Never has the cry for peace and justice so been raised among the inhabitants of this planet. They cry for help and the Bahá'ís try to answer it, since the Bahá'í investment in security derives from dedication of soul, not from the possession of personal property.

Religions mean opposing things to different people. Thus, we have seen Christians fighting Christians in two World Wars. In Viet-Nam, Buddhism to many has meant opposition to the controlling government. The dreadful reality is that man's faith in God has been crippled and there has been widespread defection to false Gods.

Christianity has existed on this planet for nearly two thousand years and yet it has some six hundred variations of its original teachings, or denominations, in America alone. This can never happen with the Bahá'í Faith. Although a few Bahá'ís—as happens with every religion—have broken away from Bahá'u'lláh's undiluted teachings and attempted to establish their own version or interpretation, invariably they have found their efforts shriveled away to nothing but bitterness.

To Bahá'ís, religion is the Life and Teachings of the Messenger. Since Bahá'u'lláh, unlike preceeding prophets, left His son. 'Abdu'l-Bahá, as Interpreter of His Teachings, the Bahá'ís hope to exclude the errors of human definition, ceremony, and ritualistic practice from their beliefs.

If the purpose of every revealed religion is considered, then that of Judaism was to teach concepts of divine law, Christianity to teach a relationship between God, man, and salvation, Islám to teach submission to the Will of God, and the Bahá'ís feel their Faith is here to bring unity to mankind and to demonstrate the unity of all the divine prophets and religions.

The Bahá'ís feel that differences happen between religions only as the result of changes made by successive prophets, and this in turn is due to the changing needs of the societies into which each prophet came, and to the subsequent interpretations and dogma added to their words by fallible religious leaders.

Even when the teachings of one past divine prophet differ from those of another, the Bahá'ís feel the difference is only surface and that in all the important things they are in complete agreement, bringing new things for the needs of the age in which each new prophet appears.

All prophetic teachings are divided into two parts. The first, with its unalterable but essential principles of love, peace, unity, and cooperation becomes renewed as divine commands through every religious cycle, and the second part, with its external practices of diet, marriage, and other laws, conforms to the requirements of its age.

Since the Bahá'í Faith actually started in 1844, with the announcement of the Forerunner of the Faith, known as the Báb (the Gate), that there would be after Him One Whom God Would Make Manifest, it is comforting to the Bahá'ís to know that they have lived in complete integration ever since, because prejudice of any kind—racial, national, class, religious, or any other—is forbidden. That is why today, when world-wide strife and racial tensions and outbreaks in the United States might startle others, the Bahá'ís rely on their belief that their purpose on earth is to know and to love God, since their Faith has the Plan to restore harmony eventually to the universe.

This is proven by the evidences of mass acceptance of the Bahá'í teachings in such currently ravaged parts of the world as Haiti, Viet-Nam, India, Africa, where new adherents to this young Faith are proclaiming their acceptance by the hundreds, often the thousands. There is not a corner or part of the world today where there is not to be found at least one Bahá'í, and many areas increase their totals so quickly that the Bahá'í International Headquarters in Haifa, Israel, cannot keep up with the constantly changing statistics.

The history of the Bahá'í Faith, however, is no different basically from that of any other true religion. The history of religion, itself, is filled with martyrdom and sacrifice. Because of the quarrels fought in the Name of God, Bahá'u'lláh has stressed that religion should be the cause of love and unity and harmony, that all divinely inspired religions are one and teach the same basic truth, the Word of God.

Long before the racial outbreaks here in America these last few years the Bahá'ís insisted that discrimination would not only create such acute conflicts but that these in turn would hold men back from enjoying the results of what can be produced with freedom of thought and the other basic freedoms.

Racial tension is but one of the many facets of the spiritual ills besetting our age, of course, to poison our thinking and to leave in its wake the conflicts that now threaten to annihilate man. The root cause of all these conflicts, as far as the Bahá'ís are concerned, has been man's refusal to apply spiritual law to his human relationships. The decline of the great religions is proof of this, the manner in which they have branched out into cults and sects because they cannot agree even on the basic truths. Religions have been so divided and subdivided that their subsequent weakness has at times even been the ruination of a specific belief. However, by applying the intellectual idea of evolution to religion, there is a plausible explanation of sorts for such dissipation and weakening and an automatic comprehension of why something newer is needed for every new age.

For instance, in Judaism, Moses brought a divine message to an undeveloped people. They would never have understood the meaning of such principles as brotherhood of man, or world peace, since there was no comprehension of world boundaries as we know them today. Therefore Moses taught them what they could understand and use for the day in which they lived—ideas of justice, for instance, the law of an eye for an eye, and of obedience to Commandments.

Later, Christ came to the descendants of these people. They had progressed so he brought them the seeds of love and neighborliness, in the belief that they would soon be ready for even higher ideals.

Six centuries later Muhammad came to extremely benighted pagans, summoning them to surrender to God. He gave his teachings to a few barbarian tribes and started them on their way toward building a great civilization.

Thus we can see that just as the cycle of Moses grew, it also reached its climax and declined. Think of it in relation to penicillin. Many people cannot tolerate repeated doses of penicillin. They need something different, a newer and stronger "wonder" drug. The system becomes used to one medication and requires another, if the illness persists.

People become tired, even bored, with the same "old" catechism. It has to be "dressed up" or "changed." They have to be given their medicine in a different way, and it is no different with spiritual ills. The world has always perked up when it has been visited by a divine teacher. Perhaps not during his lifetime, but eventually. And then, people have forgotten what he told them, or they have made it a lifeless routine, leaving out the divine spark. So, another teacher comes, knowing he need not repeat the same lines, but adding to them, as the teacher in class adds to the knowledge of the kindergarten class with grade-school lessons, and ad infinitum.

This is the way we may conceive of each religion, even though divinely inspired, as passing at some time the peak of its effectiveness, until the world prays and waits for an even greater religion to lead it ahead once more.

Today mankind is supposed to have become spiritually mature and to have developed enough to realize that religious faith is not enough without some world-encompassing principles. It may seen odd to the uninitiated that the Bahá'í Faith lacks many of the outer signs that have become tradition in other religions. There are no paid clergy, no ritualistic forms of worship apart from the reading of prayers and their Divine Writings, no formalized "do's" and "do-not's" in the manner of worship, and yet Bahá'ís *do* worship regularly.

Instead the Bahá'ís have a social principle which binds its members into a world-wide community, it has its teachings with the answers to economic, personal, and other problems, and it has a number of principles which help to bring religion together with the rest of each believer's life so that the Bahá'í teachings collectively represent the Bahá'í attitude toward God as expressed in their attitude toward their fellow man.

The Bahá'í Writings say: "He is a true Bahá'í who strives by day and by night to progress and advance along the path of human endeavor, whose cherished desire is so to live and act as to enrich and illumine the world, whose source of inspiration is the essence of Divine virtue, whose aim in life is so to conduct himself as to be the cause of infinite progress . . . In this holy Dispensation . . . Faith is no mere acknowledgment of the Unity of God, but the living of a life that will manifest all the perfections and virtues implied in such belief."

Since the cornerstone of the Bahá'í teachings is the Unity of Mankind, can it really work? Can it really come to our world during our own lifetime? The Bahá'ís have proven it everywhere. In Africa, where the various tribes have been known to be constantly warring with each other, Bahá'ís from all tribes mingle together in the utmost love and cordiality.

At the London World Congress of the Bahá'ís in 1963, in Albert Hall, seven thousand Bahá'ís gathered, representing every different form of background and former belief, all joyous at being of one Faith. And in New York City, a "melting pot" that has never blended too well, the Bahá'í gatherings have no sense of individual or racial friction. They are all too intent on bringing Bahá'u'lláh's Divine Plan to life for everyone.

This unity is the hallmark of the stage which all of human society can approach. Now that nation-building has come to an end, the Bahá'ís believe that world-building is finally on its threshold of reality. Their teachings can actually provide the practical, as well as spiritual, backing for the varying problems of mankind, but they emphasize that nothing can be solved satisfactorily without it being a part of man's religious beliefs.

The Bahá'ís do not envisage a world where everyone is alike. Diversity is fine if people can otherwise agree on certain essential principles. For instance, since many agree on racial equality, then they can go a step further and perhaps agree on having a variety of races inhabiting the same country or dwelling. If they can agree on the unity of religions, then the next step is to live in peace with all religions, even though not accepting the religion, itself, as being for everyone.

Another reason that Bahá'ís give for the need of a world religion in *this* day and age, rather than previously, is that, before the advent of Bahá'u'lláh, no world as we know it actually existed. Thanks to this age of invention and technology, the globe has shrunk to where there is now possible rapid inter-communication, rapid transportation, and rapid acquaintance with new ideas and all kinds of peoples.

Just because some of these were never known before doesn't mean they are suspect or not acceptable. In the time of Christ, he had a limited area to traverse, and yet in nearly two thousand years his ideas have gone around the entire universe and have been accepted by many. Bahá'u'lláh's teachings and ideas have traveled so swiftly and so much farther in an even shorter time, with far greater effect, because mankind finally knows its need and its illness and many of them are openly seeking a solution.

Bahá'ís believe man is capable of almost anything. He can be extremely kind, he can be extremely cruel, and because in this period of war and strife the cruelty seems uppermost, it is obvious that man also needs ideals and that today he is openly searching for the institutions through which these ideals can be expressed. Perhaps man always has had ideals, but there may have been limited numbers of applications for them previously, so again, the removal of global barriers gives him ample room for testing them. As long as man lives there will always be this tension be-tween the good and evil in him, but each prophet of God has tried to inculcate the good by offering God's way instead of man's, in the course of each life.

However, since God is essentially unknowable, His Way can only be offered to the people through these periodic revelations of His Will through His teachers—Jesus, Muhammad, Moses, Bahá'u'lláh—who communicate to man what God desires for him.

Although the prophecies of each messenger's coming were so allegorical that they could not be understood by everyone, it was a purpose of the Manifestation to explain them, and to bring whatever else was needed in their use. Again, there is the con-dition of mankind at the time each prophet appeared. Since there just weren't enough teachers or schools to take care of everyone during the time of Jesus, it would have been impossible for him to announce a rule of compulsory education for all. When Bahá-'u'lláh came, however, He knew that this would soon be possible, and thereupon made universal education mandatory upon all followers of His Faith. As a result, Iran, the country where the Bahá'í Faith started (at which time it was called Persia) today has approximately eighty-percent illiteracy among the non-Bahá'ís, but around ninety-percent literacy among the followers of Bahá'u'lláh.

People have long recognized that the great need of the world is to return to the pure teaching of Jesus. In fact, the hearts of the nations cry out for a return of *all* the divinely revealed messengers, since their teachings manifest the eternal essence of religion, which is universal love.

In 1912, 'Abdu'l-Bahá, Bahá'u'llah's Son, visited America. A Christian minister asked Him: "How can we help this Bahá'í movement toward universal peace and brotherhood?"

'Abdu'l-Bahá replied: "Teach the pure gospel of Jesus without dogmatic additions or limitations."

During that same visit, He was asked by a university professor: "If I become a Bahá'í, can I keep the religion of my saintly Christian mother?"

"Of course you may keep it," 'Abdu'l-Bahá replied. *"If you become a Bahá'í you will apply it."*

One way in which the Bahá'ís can show their universal outlook is by having Bahá'í Houses of Worship on each of the four continents today. There is one at Wilmette, Illinois, one at Kampala, Uganda, Africa, one at Sydney, Australia, and one at Frankfurt, Germany. There is also the Shrine of the Báb at the Bahá'í International Headquarters in Haifa, Israel, on the side of Mount Carmel. These were all built with contributions from Bahá'ís only, as no contributions are sought or accepted from non-Bahá'ís for Bahá'í endeavors. If such contributions do come in voluntarily, they are used for general charitable purposes, not for Bahá'í teaching or construction.

Many religions concentrate on the "hereafter" in their teachings, and while the Bahá'ís are well aware of their souls' commitment, they are also concerned with the "here now," and with trying to bring the Kingdom of God on earth. They believe that a soul's development is actually concerned with the development of all mankind. The world is filled with various kinds of poverty but to Bahá'ís the poverty of the spirit is the worst.

Most important, however, is that the Bahá'ís feel they can accomplish the goals set for mankind by the coming of Bahá'u'lláh. These are the creation of world peace and unity among the nations of the world, not only through love but because the Bahá'ís have the special ideals, rules, and plans for making these a reality.

What the Bahá'í Plan is and how It has developed is what this book is about.

The Bahá'í
Way of Life

What Is a Bahá'í?

A BAHA'I on the surface may seem like anyone else you know who has declared his belief in God and appears to want to do the right thing. He is human, but he is also fallible. Some Bahá'ís concentrate more on the spiritual application of their teachings, ignoring the day-to-day world in which they live. Other Bahá'ís become so engrossed in the routine affairs of administration that they relegate the spiritual part of their Faith as something belonging to Holy Days, community gatherings, and public meetings.

They are both wrong, of course. The true Bahá'í is not merely enrolled in the Faith, he is confirmed into it, and he eventually learns to live simultaneously in three worlds—the Kingdom of God, the Bahá'í community, and the world of humanity. When he becomes a Bahá'í he is already so spiritually motivated through his new faith and love that whatever he does becomes a little more noble. Then to sustain his faith and to grow with it, he needs a pattern, laws and principles, and it has been to help form this pattern that the Bahá'í Administrative Order was created to be a part of the New Age for its followers.

The sincere Bahá'í does not fulfill his destiny by remaining quiet and serene in one place, bathed in the ecstasy of his love of God. He goes out and does something to demonstrate this love in deed, and usually starts out on a personal level by making changes in his own life and the manner of his association with other people.

The late Guardian of the Faith, Shoghi Effendi, writes that the connection between the worlds of God's Kingdom and the Bahá'í Administrative Order is that the former generates the vision and maintains the ardor and spirit of service, while the latter represents the specific task to be achieved. The Bahá'í task is to unite humanity in one Faith and one Order and to do this there must be unity within the Faith, as well.

The loyal Bahá'í gives his best effort to the work of the community while seeking to convey its spirit and its love to others. He learns that the laws and ordinances that may sound overwhelming at first are actually blessings from God for the establishment of the new Bahá'í society. He finds through the teachings that the Bahá'í institutions were divinely created in order to establish peace and justice upon earth and that in his associations with his fellow Bahá'ís he will have the opportunity to become part of the life of God's Kingdom.

A new Bahá'í feels reborn. He senses that he is going through the process of obtaining a new heart and mind through the development of his spiritual qualities. Some individuals arrive at these confirmations more quickly than others, but eventually each believer wins it by a combination of patient work and prayer, if he desires to win it at all.

The Bahá'í with true balance is the most fortunate of all. He lives consciously in both the spiritual and the administrative realms. His soul is at peace, neither aloof nor self-absorbed on one hand, nor immersed in petty detail on the other. Those Bahá'ís who honestly strive to establish the New World Order follow the first prerogative of a believer. They begin to teach, and no matter how little they know, they are encouraged to use this for their first teaching efforts. This is part of the Bahá'í belief that no human activity can be as rewarding spiritually as working and striving for the Faith.

'Abdu'l-Bahá's definition of a Bahá'í is someone who is "a *friend* to all religions and to all nations. I consider all of one race and count them as my relatives. I have a Divine love and not a racial or sectarian love. . . ."

"According to the explicit written command of Bahá'u'lláh," He has also stated, ". . . we are concerned with things which are heavenly. We are servants unto the world of morality. We consider that religious, racial, political, and national prejudices are destructive to the world of humanity. We believe that the whole surface of the earth constitutes our home, and all mankind one family. . . ."

One form of Bahá'í teaching is also a form of the hospitality they are all urged to practice. Small teaching meetings are called "firesides,"and are held in private homes. They enjoy having Bahá'ís or non-Bahá'ís as house-guests in their homes, to share their material possessions and love and knowledge. This is the essence of Bahá'í hospitality.

Bahá'ís are taught to try always to be truthful and reverent, to cause grief to no one, to be kind to all, and to love others with a pure spirit. They are also asked to remain silent about the faults of others, pray for them, and help them. Bahá'ís strive always to see the good in others, not the bad. If a man has ten good qualities and one bad, they are implored to overlook the bad one. If he has ten bad qualities and one good, they are urged to see only the good one.

Bahá'ís believe that when they concern themselves with the broad vision of life, the rest will follow. What might not be a likable attribute in a fellow believer may be the very quality that enables him to do his best work. The same rationalizing seems to work with personalities that might ordinarily conflict. The one who is slow to understand and holds things up during a discussion may be the one to have extra sound judgment when given time to ponder, or may possess a highly retentive memory. The person who seems not too clever may still possess an inordinate spiritual quality that will have a pleasing effect upon others.

The emotional individual can often get out valuable work quickly that would not even be attempted by the dignified one. Bahá'ís learn to see what is valuable in each person. They are taught to forego criticism, omit fault-finding and backbiting, to refrain from hasty judgments and not to anticipate insincere motives, but first to secure all the facts of a situation.

These are merely some of the aids for a new believer which can enable him to become a true member of the Bahá'í community and the Bahá'í life.

The Bahá'í Community

ONE PRINCIPLE underlying the administration of the affairs of the Bahá'í Faith is aimed at improving the life and building up the character of each individual believer. Bahá'í authority in their administration is not given or elected in order to enhance the personal prestige of those who by appointment or election are assigned to positions of seeming higher authority. Bahá'í authority is measured by self-sacrifice and service, not by arbitrary power.

The local Bahá'í community is given official status only after its number of adult declared believers, aged twenty-one or over, has become nine or more. Before this, if there is only one Bahá'í in a locality he is known as an isolated believer, and from two to eight are called a group. Each group, of course, aims at growing into a full-fledged Bahá'í community of nine or more, since nine persons are necessary for the formation of a Local Spiritual Assembly.

Since each group is the reservoir from which the future Local Assembly will be formed, each group membership challenges the individual believer to begin trying to live the Bahá'í life and to demonstrate to nonbelievers the potency of the Faith of Bahá'u'-lláh. It obliges the individual Bahá'í to attain accord and harmony with his fellow believers and he learns about the power of Bahá'í consultation in anything that affects the group as a whole. Such consultations and joint decisions by majority vote of the group members help them to prepare for their later experience as members of the Local Spiritual Assembly, and as members of a full-fledged Bahá'í community.

It is by carrying out successful teaching activities, and learning how to consult cooperatively with, but not in personal subjugation to, their fellow Bahá'ís that gradually new Bahá'ís hope to acquire emotional stability, courage, self-respect and mental clarity along with a knowledge of the basic Bahá'í teachings, the nature of the Administrative Order and the progress of the Bahá'í World Crusade.

They learn that it is not by force of numbers or the mere exposition of a set of new and noble principles or other high ideals that they can hope to achieve the goals set for Bahá'ís throughout the universe. The late Guardian wrote that "one thing and only one thing will unfailingly and alone secure the undoubted triumph of this sacred Cause, namely, the extent to which our own inner life and private character mirror forth in their manifold aspects the splendor of those eternal principles proclaimed by Bahá'u'lláh. . . ."

When a Bahá'í group becomes nine or more, it elects a Local Spiritual Assembly and acquires official recognition as a community. The word "community" in the Bahá'í sense is not a reference to area locality or any manner of living that differs from what other people have, or the general environment such as has been attempted by other religious, philosophic, and even economic enthusiasts of the past.

A Bahá'í community is more a matter of unity of minds and hearts, in the association of people who are equally devoted to promoting the universal aims of their beliefs, and are all in full agreement as to the methods by which these aims can be advanced. Their association is purely voluntary, no one is permitted to force anyone to "become" a Bahá'í, and since the methods by which the aims of the Faith can be advanced are all part of the Bahá'í teachings, they are no different for one believer than another.

Someone who is attracted to the Bahà'ì Faith finds that he is on the threshold of a new spiritual experience. He learns that God loves those who work in groups and that His chief purpose in this age is to create unity. To do his part in building a New World Order, each person has to develop new qualities of character, which the Bahá'ís feel their teachings demonstrate.

The seeker learns that the Bahá'í Faith is not a church. It does not have a formal creed to be recited, or sacraments, or a clergy. It is not a denomination of Christianity or Islam or Judaism. It is a religious community, composed of laws, principles and institutions for community life. This life is based on the spirit of cooperation and cooperation means that two attitudes, very strong in American life, are actually harmful in the Bahá'í Faith. The first is that of "having to run the show." The second is that of "letting George do it." In churches the minister is paid to do the study and spiritual reflection for the members; he is also largely responsible for many practical affairs. In the Bahá'í Faith the members have a continuing responsibility for deepening their knowledge in the teachings of Bahá'u'lláh. Each member of a Local Assembly shares with eight other people the administrative responsibility for the Faith in that town or city. If appointed on a committee, each member again has the shared responsibility with others. Under all circumstances, there is always opportunity for believers to cooperate and do their share in the great Bahá'í enterprise of building the Kingdom of God upon earth.

A declaration of Bahá'í faith may be made anywhere, at any time, in the presence of any Bahá'í or group of Bahá'ís, through the mail, or over the telephone. The Bahá'í or Bahá'ís to whom the declaration is made should provide the person with a Bahá'í registration card (available to all Bahá'ís in good standing). Signing this card constitutes the formal declaration. The occasion

is made into a special event by the Bahá'ís who know the declarant, and there is much joy and love and rejoicing evident. After
the card has been properly filled out by the declarant, it is given
or sent to the administrative body for enrolling him in that area,
together with either a statement from the declarant about his
knowledge and acceptance of Bahá'u'lláh, or a report from his
Bahá'í teacher, if a Bahá'í teacher has been involved.

The final procedure of formal enrollment into the Bahá'í
community is effected after the administrative body has countersigned his registration card and forwarded it to the national office
along with the regulation membership report form. For the most
part, national approval is automatic and the declarant may attend
Bahá'í functions immediately after the local administrative body
has countersigned his membership card, which he receives even
before the other forms go to the national headquarters.

Many local administrative bodies and even applicants for
Bahá'í membership are warmed by the suggestions given by the
Hands of the Cause in the Holy Land (see the chapter beginning
on page 133 for explanation of "Hands") in this message of
April 1962.

> Those who declare themselves as Bahá'ís should become
> enchanted with the beauty of the Teachings, and touched by
> the love of Bahá'u'lláh. The declarants need not know all the
> proofs, history, laws, and principles of the Faith, but in the
> process of declaring themselves they must, in addition to
> catching the spark of faith, become basically informed about
> the Central Figures of the Faith, as well as the existence of
> laws they must follow and an administration they must obey.

As the new Bahá'í studies, he recognizes that obedience to
Bahá'u'lláh includes citizenship in His World Order. It means
the new Bahá'í must be sincere in his acceptance, also, of the
Báb and 'Abdu'l-Bahá, as set forth in 'Abdu'lBaha's Last Will
and Testament. He agrees to accept and submit to whatever
laws and regulations of the Supreme Legislative Body, the
Universal House of Justice, are currently applicable; and to

loyally and steadfastly adhere to their Instructions and Directives. He associates with the spirit as well as with the form
of the present-day Bahá'í administration throughout the world
and by so doing becomes obedient to any other mandates or
doctrines offered by the present-day Supreme Body, the Universal
House of Justice, in its past, present, or future deliberations.

Each Bahá'í recognizes that the Institutions he is helping to
establish now can assure tomorrow's world of the peace to which
all mankind aspires. Since these Institutions are Divine in origin,
they are based upon spiritual principles which are unchangeable.
Legal Bahá'í administrative decisions cannot go beyond the spiritual laws which are supposed to be expressed in them, but the
procedure used to create these decisions is flexible so as to conform to the current needs, but make certain such decisions represent the spirit of justice, the will to demonstrate love, and a
consideration of the good of all in their results.

The individuals in a Bahá'í community are not elected to a
Local Spiritual Assembly to represent a part of the community.
The nine members are there to work in unity, think of the good of
the entire community, and to consider themselves as nine parts
of the whole, not as nine individuals.

When a decision affecting Bahá'í welfare—individual or
community—is required, this is done through the Bahá'í procedure of consultation. Two or more persons involved consult
together or, if necessary, with the Local Assembly, in order to
be guided by a discussion set in a spirit of good will and mutual
understanding.

This delicate task is something for which Bahá'ís are patiently
and lovingly trained through individual progression into the
Bahá'í way and attitude. It requires tact and often the art of
being firm without appearing acrimonious. Consultation of this
sort is only possible when each participant accepts the discipline
of pooling his opinion when asked for it, and then *forgetting* it.
Bahá'ís are taught that once they have prayerfully and objectively
considered the aspects of a situation or problem and have given

their opinion or thoughts on it, that opinion is no longer theirs, it belongs to Bahá'u'lláh and through Him to God.

Whether their individual opinions have been accepted in making up the majority decision is not important. Once it *has* been made, then any contrary opinions no longer exist. The Baha'í or Bahá'ís who originally felt differently about the matter must accept and act upon the final decision as though it was their own way of thinking from the start. They are taught that if the decision is wrong that eventually Bahá'u'lláh will straighten out the matter.

The sincere Bahá'í learns that such "radiant acquiescence" isn't as difficult as it sounds. It is merely a matter of giving up one's opinion to God. If a Bahá'í does that, there is nothing left to feel personal about. The only aim of proper Bahá'í consultation is to work out a decision for the good of the Faith, in an atmosphere reflecting the ideal of love, common action, unity, so that the participants will remain on a high spiritual plane during the discussion.

If nations could follow this Bahá'í pattern, it might not be as difficult as one might imagine to envision the establishment of peace and harmony for the future of mankind.

The Bahá'í Life — Its Laws, Morals, Ordinances, and Obligations

FOR EVERYTHING the obedient Bahá'í does—or wants to do—in his daily life, there is a specific prerequisite, answer, or pattern in the Bahá'í Writings. In the United States, for instance, where the individual states have so much confusion regarding marriage and divorce, there is no confusion for the Bahá'ís. They have it all spelled out in close detail.

The marriage of a Bahá'í—whether to another Bahá'í or a non-Bahá'í—is meant to express the spiritual, as well as physical, uniting of the couple so that they will continue to have eternal unity throughout all the divine worlds and improve each other's personal life here and spiritual life through time to come. They are taught that when relationship, union, and concord exist between a couple from both the physical and spiritual standpoint, that is the real union and one that is everlasting. Should the union be merely from the physical point of view, unquestionably it is merely temporal; and unless it becomes spiritual, separation is usually inevitable.

The precise requirements of Bahá'í marriage in the United States are:

1. The young couple must choose each other freely.

2. The living parents of both—whether or not they are Bahá'ís —must give their consent to the marriage in writing or before credible witnesses. This is necessary regardless of how old the "children" involved may be.

3. In a state where a civil ceremony is also necessary, a Bahá'í ceremony must be performed on the same day, except in instances where legitimate exception has been permitted by the National Assembly.

A Bahá'í marriage ceremony is very simple and beautiful. The basic requirement is that the bride and groom utter the statement of Bahá'í belief, "we will all verily abide by the Will of God." This statement, uttered by the couple in the presence of officially designated witnesses of the Bahá'í community, is all that is required by the Local Assembly, since marriage is a Local Spiritual Assembly function. Although this is all that is essential, the reading of several of the prayers given for marriage in the prayer book helps to complete the Bahá'í ceremony beautifully with its nobility of thoughts and beauty of language regarding the marriage state.

Many people are interested in the Bahá'í attitude concerning marriage to a non-Bahà'ì. If a Bahà'ì marries a non-Bahà'í who wishes to have the religious ceremony of his own sect carried out, it must be quite clear that, first, the Bahá'í partner is understood to be a Bahá'í by religion, and will not accept the religion of the other party to the marriage through having his or her religious ceremony; and second, the ceremony must be of a nature which does not commit the Bahá'í to any declaration of faith in a religion other than his own. Under these circumstances, the Bahá'í can partake of the religious ceremony of his non-Bahá'í partner. If there are two ceremonies, one for the non-Bahá'í's religion the Bahá'í ceremony must be held on the same day.

Concerning the dissolution of a marriage, Bahá'u'lláh makes it clear to his followers that divorce in general is to be deplored even though it is permissible. There is no guilt attached to divorce per se, though acts which may be at the root of marital break-up may sometimes be considered unworthy. Bahá'u'lláh gave explicit instructions on everything possible and expressed them plainly but emphatically. His teachings make the obtaining of a divorce something that would not be hasty or ill-advised, by including suggestions for possible re-establishment of the marriage bond. During Bahá'í divorce proceedings He has set standards of behavior which allow the preservation of honor and Bahá'í decorum on the part of both people involved, if those standards are honestly adhered to.

By following the Bahá'í divorce procedures, a great deal of suffering and heartbreak is eliminated or reduced. The procedures provide sufficient time for the carrying out of many steps toward possible reconciliation of the unhappy couple, renewing their understanding, healing their wounds, even restoring their love for each other. They also help to resolve any economic, social, and family problems which a long-established marriage has created, when a divorce seems necessary.

The basic rule for securing all this is called the Bahá'í Year of Patience. The Year of Patience is precisely that—a full year in which a man and his wife patiently try to resolve their difficulties in their marriage. At the time one or both parties go before the Local Spiritual Assembly to announce their disagreement, the Assembly usually accepts that as the date of the start of the official year, during which the couple must live under separate roofs, although the period of time is planned as the start of reconciliation attempts.

The Assembly very lovingly acts as mediator for the couple, and, if necessary, can refer them to professional marriage counselors as well. To further the possible chance of a reconciliation, the couple is not supposed to "date" others during that year, nor are they to act in any way as though they are not still married, except for the fact of living apart physically. They are to have no more than the normal public contact with others of the opposite sex, and extramarital sexual relations are certainly forbidden. If the man and wife at any time have sexual relations with each other during the year, this is considered a form of reconciliation, and should they agree to disagree the very next day, however, the Local Assembly would still consider that the amount of time already counted as part of the year of patience had been nullified, and a new year of patience would have to commence.

In brief, that year is intended as a time of complete physical separation for the couple, of re-examination of the true foundations of their marriage and of consideration of the potential for its resumption. This potential can be resolved by the reconcilation of the couple at any time during the year.

Should the year elapse without resumption of the marriage ties or resolution of the couple's marital problems, the Bahá'í divorce is final and is accepted as final by the Bahá'í community. Civil devorce can follow, but afterwards the man and women should show greater friendship and appreciation toward each other than before their separation.

Bahá'ís also have laws which forbid gambling, the use of narcotics, and the imbibing of alcoholic beverages. Even moderate drinking is felt to be a serious reflection upon the Faith, since the Bahá'ís are known as complete abstainers. It is not an accident that Bahá'u'lláh prohibited alcohol, and it is easy to adduce extensive evidence to indicate certain of the hazards of alcohol, particularly when people undergo stresses and many seem to rely upon alcohol for courage or support. The same attitude applies to narcotics. In Bahá'u'lláh's teachings their use is recognized as dangerous, threatening to many social relations, and no substitute for the pillars of religious and social life.

On the other hand, while smoking is frowned upon, there is no Bahá'í law actually forbidding it. For the same reason that certain things are forbidden to Bahá'ís because the preservation of individual health and independence are required, for many years (long before many scientists announced their own findings in various governmental health surveys) 'Abdu'l-Bahá told the believers that the smoking of tobacco is unclean, malodorous, disagreeable, and vulgar and can cause gradual harm to the smoker.

Bahá'ís are also required to refrain from participation in partisan activities, to withdraw from membership in churches and ecclesiastical organizations or certain secret ones, such as the Masons. Shoghi Effendi sharply advised the American Bahá'ís to "shun politics like the plague and be obedient to the government in power in the place where you reside. . . ."

Today the Bahá'ís face the fact that society has disintegrated so rapidly that moral issues which were clear a half century ago have become hopelessly confused.. What is worse, the issues have become thoroughly mixed up with battling political interests. Bahá'ís fear they would become lost if they become involved in the issues the governments of different people are struggling over. However, if they build up the Bahá'í pattern in each country, they can offer it as a remedy when all else has failed.

At various times, the Guardian has also instructed the believers:

> . . . bearing on the controversial and political issues of the day . . . while endeavoring to uphold loyally and expound . . . our social and moral principles in all their essence and purity . . . refusing to utter the word that would needlessly alienate or estrange any individual, government or people, we should fearlessly and unhesitatingly uphold and assert in their

entirety such truths the knowledge of which we believe is vitally and urgently needed for the good and betterment of mankind.

We should every one of us remain aloof, in heart and mind, in words and deeds from political affairs and disputes of Nations and Governments.

The friends may vote, if they can do it, without identifying themselves with one party or another. . . . It remains for the individuals to so use their right to vote as to keep aloof from party politics, and to always bear in mind that they are voting on the merits of the individual, rather than because he belongs to one party or another. . . .

The Bahá'í system is unique. With all Bahá'í adult citizens eligible and enjoined to vote in Bahá'í elections, there is no party, only an electorate, with no electioneering and no nominations. The balloting is secret, with authority and power vested in assemblies of the annually elected. There is no priesthood and no professional leadership. Bahá'í consultation is channeled into decision through God's methods, and with the Bahá'í community pledged to unity in action, the individual Bahá'ís must still live and interact with contemporary life. In the American democracy they contribute as citizens but only in limited ways.

Bahá'ís may vote if they do not identify themselves with a particular political party. They must be individuals and remain aloof from party politics. They are cautioned to keep in mind that they are voting for the merits of an individual, not for the party to which he belongs. In this way Bahá'ís are free to exercise their personal discretion and judgment when choosing those for whom they vote, since they vote as nonpartisan independents. However, they are not permitted to vote in primaries where to cast a ballot would call for a partisan choice and identify the Bahá'ís as voting for a party member.

There are other limitations. "No Bahá'ís vote for an office," they are told in their teachings, "no Bahá'í's participation in the affairs of the Republic, shall involve acceptance . . . of a program or policy that contravenes any vital principle, spiritual or social, of the Faith."

In addition: "No vote cast, or office undertaken, by a Bahá'í should necessarily constitute acceptance by the voter or office holder of the entire program of any political party."

No Bahá'í can be regarded as a member of *any* political party, large or small. A Bahá'í is above all else the "supporter of the principles enunciated by Bahá'u'lláh with which . . . the program of no political party is completely harmonious."

'Abdu'l-Bahá has written:

> . . . the Cause of God is withdrawn entirely from political affairs; the political realm pertains only to the Rulers of those matters; it has nothing to do with the souls who are exerting their utmost energy to harmonizing affairs, helping character and inciting [the people] to strive for perfection. Therefore no soul is allowed to interfere with [political] matters, but only in that which is commanded . . .

The concerns of thinking people are many. Although Bahá'ís are cautioned to avoid being aligned with any political figures publicly—either pro or con—or to avoid writing or discussing matters bearing upon the political issues of the day, they are well aware that too narrow an interpretation by them of "politics" might serve to shut the doors of association with others whose world interests might bring a coalition of ideas that would eventually stimulate recognition of the ideas of the Faith from many directions.

Although Bahá'ís are obliged to refrain from association with any subversive movement, and are not allowed to accept any political office by vote of a political party, they may still accept nonpolitical public appointments or civil service in governments where partisan commitments are neither implied nor demanded.

Bahá'ís have a cardinal principle of being obedient to the government prevailing in the country in which Bahá'ís reside.

Regardless of the form of government, or their personal instincts against it, they are forbidden to join underground movements seeking to overthrow the government in power.

However, Bahá'ís are not permitted to judge *how* a particular government came into power or whether or not it should be obeyed. That, again, would be plunging the Faith into politics. Once there is a legal government, regardless of the methods employed to establish that legality, the Bahá'ís must obey its directives in everything except matters where spiritual Bahá'í principle is involved. Such a principle would be apparent if the government banned the Faith or asked Bahá'ís to deny it, and for such spiritual principles sincerely devout Bahá'ís would willingly accept any punishment or recourse from the government, even death.

In view of this idea of obedience to one's government, the matter of military service naturally comes to mind.

Since Bahá'ís abhor any duties that necessitate the taking of life, it is obligatory, not optional, for all Bahá'ís in the United States to apply for noncombatant military status when registering at the age of eighteen. By registering as a Bahá'í there is opportunity, also, for the individual Bahá'í to help to have his Faith recognized both by the Draft Board and among acquaintances. Instructions for Bahá'í youth and the Bahá'í statements on military service and loyalty to government are supplied believers at the proper time.

All Bahá'í males in the United States are sent the Bahá'í explanation of their military service when they reach military age, by the National Assembly of Bahá'ís of the United States. If they are older when they declare themselves, it is included in their welcome to the Faith from the National Assembly.

A person who becomes a Bahá'í while in uniform, and who does not already have noncombatant status has an obligation to the government to finish out his term of duty, the Bahá'í administration feels. However, it may be possible to obtain de facto noncombatant status by transferring to a selected duty which does not call for physical fighting. Such a transfer should be effected in a way that will not impair the Bahá'í member's relationships with his responsible superiors, he is advised, and should leave no question of his willingness to serve his country without regard for personal safety, comfort, or type of service to which he may be assigned.

Bahá'í servicemen are asked to request identification as Bahá'í, not as Protestant, Catholic, or Jew.

Although in most military funerals burial is near the place of death, it is more difficult in nonmilitary funerals to follow this precept. However, all Bahá'ís must specify that their burial cannot be more than one hour's journey from the place of death, and that the body cannot or should not be cremated or embalmed unless a state law requires either of these procedures.

Certain of the Bahá'í laws and ordinances are considered between the individual believer and God, or his conscience. Among those are his duty to teach the Faith, saying the obligatory daily prayer; keeping the annual fast; attendance at the Nineteen-Day Feast; contributing regularly to the Bahá'í Funds and leaving a written will and testament; and, if he is able, engaging in a useful trade or profession.

The obligatory laws which require complete obedience to the Institutions of the Faith include those on marriage and divorce, those forbidding gambling and the imbibing of alcholic beverages and narcotics and those regarding political affiliations. Any disobedience of these laws is subject to administrative action and can result in disciplinary measures being invoked, which could include the loss of Bahá'í voting rights or other Bahá'í membership privileges.

Two obligations for Bahá'ís may be unfamiliar to other religious affiliations. One is unique and called the Nineteen-Day Feast. The other is the Bahá'í obligation to leave a written will and testament.

To explain the Nineteen-Day Feast requires an explanation of the Bahá'í Calendar. History has no record of any society which has ever for a considerable period followed a calendar established by civil authority. The testimony of human experience seems to have proven without exception that people measure time and record dates according to a calendar based upon specific appearances of the Manifestation of God. Many different methods over the centuries have been adopted for this purpose. Several different calendars are still in frequent use, as many may well know: the Gregorian Calendar in Western Europe, the Julian Calendar in many countries of Eastern Europe, and the Hebrew Calendar among the Jews, plus the Muḥammadan Calendar in Muslim countries.

When the Báb was inspired to emphasize the importance of His Dispensation, He signalized its advent with a new calendar in which, as in the Gregorian Calendar, the lunar month is abandoned and the solar year is adopted. The Bahá'í year consists of nineteen months of nineteen days each, with the addition of certain "intercalary days" (four in ordinary, five in leap years) between the eighteenth and nineteenth month. The Báb named the months after the attributes of God. Splendor, Glory, Beauty, Light, Perfection, Might, and Will are some. Similarly the days of the week are named Glory, Beauty, Perfection, Grace, Justice, Majesty, and Independence.

This new division of the days into months completes the full cycle of the earth's revolution around the sun in the Bahá'í chronology and inaugurates a new social rhythm whose full implications cannot yet be realized, but which connotes to the Bahá'ís a new economics, a new and better way of life.

Intercalary Days, although neither Feast nor Anniversary, are days of hospitality, charity, and the giving of gifts. Bahá'ís do not observe such holidays as Christmas and New Year in relation to each other, and their festival gatherings are held instead at their New Year (Naw-Rúz) and during the Intercalary Days.

The Bahá'í New Year, like the ancient Persian New Year, is astronomically fixed, commencing at the March equinox. The Bahá'í Era began with the year of the Báb's Declaration in 1844. The Intercalary Days are followed by nineteen days of fasting, consisting of abstinence from food and drink from sunrise to sunset for nineteen days. The believers rise before sunrise to pray and eat breakfast. In places where the days and nights vary, they approximate the hours of sunrise and sunset elsewhere. The fast concludes with the Bahá'í New Year at sunset on March 20, on the vernal equinox.

The Bahá'ís believe that in the not far distant future it will be necessary for all people in the world to agree on a common calendar, one free from the objections and associations which make each of the older calendars unacceptable to large segments of the world's population. It is difficult to figure how any other calendar arrangement could exceed in simplicity and convenience the one devised by the Báb.

As a point of explanation here, the number "9" singly or as part of "19" appears frequently in Bahá'í lore. Bahá'ís revere the number "9" because (1) it is a sign of perfection, hence symbolizes comprehensiveness, culmination, and (2) it is the numerical value of the word "Bahá" (in numerology connected with the Arabic alphabet) and is the Name of the Revealer of the Bahá'í Faith—Bahá'u'lláh.

The Institution of the Nineteen-Day Feast was ordained by Bahá'u'lláh for Bahá'ís only, and is unique. It is looked forward to as a time of loving reunion by community members and Bahá'í friends. If a member is out of town on a feast date he usually seeks out one being held where he is visiting.

The Feast is held on the first day of the Bahá'í month. It consists of three parts arranged to merge into a unity. The first part is devotional, consisting of prayers and reading from the Bahá'í Writings. The second part, which is the consultation and "business" portion, includes Bahá'í committee reports, matters and correspondence from their National Assembly or the Universal House of Justice, and submission of suggestions or even problems from the community which require discussion and consultation. The third part is social, where the friends relax together, usually over some light form of refreshment.

The Local Assembly secretary during the business part of the

Feast reports on decisions made by that body since the last Feast, and takes down any suggestions made by believers at the current feast for the Assembly to consider at its future meetings. The members of Bahá'í community have the right to discuss frankly any question raised during consultation and to offer ideas and recommendations for their Assembly's future consideration.

The Bahá'í Feast is intended as a joyful occasion, the rallying point of the entire community. There is Bahá'í music, Bahá'í love, and the happiness of being together at least every nineteen days. New Bahá'ís are welcomed, members transferred from other communities are welcomed, and visiting Bahá'ís from elsewhere are welcomed. Spontaneous loving greetings flow as those present become caught up in the atmosphere of spiritual and consultative unity, and it is a time when the true Bahá'í spirit is emphasized over and over.

The late Guardian described the Institution of the Nineteen-Day Feast as "the foundation of the World Order of Bahá'u'lláh. . . . Bahá'ís should regard [it] as the very heart of their spiritual activity . . . their steadfast unity with one another in a mystery raised high above the limitations of race, class, nationality, sect, and personality, and their privilege of contributing to the power of the Cause in the realm of collective action. "

Another matter of personal conscience is the obligation for a Bahá'í to leave a written will and testament stating how his property is to be disposed of after his death. The reasoning behind this is that people take great care of their assets while alive, but are frequently careless or indifferent when it comes to the equally important protection of this same property after death.

There is also the logic that, should a believer want any portion of his estate to go to the Faith, in some states his wishes would be disregarded unless left in a written will. A will is also important regarding the believer's instructions for Bahá'í burial, proper disposition of his Bahá'í books and literature, files and records, and Bahá'í education for his children.

Inherent in the idea of providing for the Faith is the matter that living Bahá'ís have responsibility to the various Bahá'í Funds. In an age of solicitation, raffles, and benefits which bribe contribution by the promise of self-enrichment, the Bahá'ís are unique by initiating and holding to a standard of maturity in their emphasis upon *voluntary* financial support accepted only from declared believers.

No individual Bahá'í is exposed to scorn or ridicule for failure to render financial support to his Faith. Contributions are confidential, usually known only to the treasurer of the local, national, or international funds, except when for some special administrative reason the local, national, or international body requests information about a believer's contributions.

The Bahá'í Faith does not separate the devotion of contribution from the devotion of prayer and feels that both have the same dignity and the same obligations. Any financial appeal is usually made in Bahá'í publications or at Nineteen-Day Feasts, especially for funds to help fulfill certain building or teaching goals. Always, the money has been forthcoming, even during the early stages when there were fewer believers and the appeal may have taken longer to be fulfilled or answered.

Many Bahá'ís make great personal sacrifices to meet the obligations inherent with Bahá'í membership, yet none are singled out as representing the best example of generosity. Some may do it with money, others with their time or services and many do it by traveling to other cities, even other countries, as Pioneers. Not everyone can leave his home area to be a Pioneer for the Faith, because of family responsibilities. Those who cannot travel themselves are urged to help pay the expense of the teachers with time and energy, but not the necessary funds.

In writing of the proper Bahá'í attitude about giving, Shoghi Effendi has explained:

We must be like the fountain or spring that is continually emptying itself of all that it has and is continually being refilled from an invisible source. To be continually giving out for the good of our fellows undeterred by the fear of poverty and reliant on the unfailing bounty of the Source of all wealth and all good—this is the secret of right living.

The Bahá'ís, as previously stated, do not accept contributions from nonmembers for any of their buildings, goals, or activities. No plates are passed around for contributions at Bahá'í meetings or public meetings. No function is held to help a Bahá'í activity in which a non-Bahá'í is asked to pay admission. If Bahá'ís want to pay for non-Bahá'ís to be their guests, this is permitted.

Many times, grateful non-Bahá'í families with a loved one who had been a Bahá'í and had a Bahá'í funeral will send in a small contribution. The Local Spiritual Assembly can use it for a non-Bahá'í charitable fund, such as the Red Cross, or it may be sent to the National Assembly, which has its own charities.

The Bahá'í Moral Code

THE BAHA'I LIFE is not merely a matter of the ordinances, laws, and obligations which are so obvious. Bahá'ís also have the individual and concerted responsibility to endeavor constantly each day to be examples of the highest standards of the Faith in their lives, their conduct, and their associations, and to be loving to each other, as well as to those around them.

Bahá'ís are required to lead a chaste and holy life, to be modest, pure, temperate, decent, and clean-minded, and to involve a constant exercise of moderation in dress, language, amusements, and any artistic or literary work they may undertake. They have to control their desires and inclinations so as not to be carnal or corrupt, and to observe a lack of frivolity or to omit excessive attachment to trivial or what may be misdirected pleasures. Their Faith condemns the prostitution of art and of literature, the practices of nudism and of companionate marriage, marital infidelity, and all manner of promiscuity, easy familiarity, and sexual vices.

They are not supposed to tolerate any compromise with their beliefs despite the demands of a modern age, and must demonstrate through their own lives the Bahá'í belief that present-day theories are pernicious, current standards are generally false, and undue excesses are, frankly, sacrilegious.

"By the righteousness of God!" Bahá'u'lláh has instructed, "the world, its vanities and its glory, and whatever delights it can offer, are all in the sight of God, as worthless as, nay even more contemptible than, dust and ashes. Would that the hearts of men could comprehend it. Wash yourselves thoroughly, O people of Bahá, from the defilement of the world, and of all that pertaineth unto it. God Himself beareth Me witness! The things of the earth ill beseem you. . . . Advance into the vast immensity of the realm of God, and abide ye in the meads of sanctity and detachment. . . ."

Bahá'ís are enjoined in every way possible to be a good example to all, and to reflect in their own actions the teachings of the Faith they follow. If a believer slips from the path of rectitude, it is not for his fellow believers to become either judge or jury. This is an administrative matter, and all such instances come under the immediate province of Local Spiritual Assemblies. An Assembly is asked to decide, in consultation, just how flagrant the believer's action was, the word "flagrant" being protection against minor complaints or picayune personal considerations of each other's actions, which Bahá'ís are also warned against instigating.

The Bahá'í standard is not to be confused or associated with asceticism, or excessive and bigoted puritanism simply because Bahá'ís are trying to maintain a high standard of moral conduct for themselves.

"Should a man," Bahá'u'lláh writes reassuringly, "wish to adorn himself with the ornaments of the earth, to wear its apparels, or partake of the benefits it can bestow, no harm can befall him, if he alloweth nothing whatever to intervene between him and God, for God hath ordained every good thing, whether created in the heavens or in the earth, for such of His servants as truly believe in Him. Eat, O people, of the good things which God hath allowed you, and deprive not yourselves from His wondrous bounties. Render thanks and praise unto Him, and be of them that are truly thankful."

Therefore, Bahá'ís can acquire wealth, and position, but they are expected to remember the needs and cautions of the Faith so as not to flaunt material possessions. Bahá'ís know their money is not meant to be displayed or dispensed profligately. Even if they cannot or do not give all of their free time and extra earnings directly to the Faith, the manner in which they use this time or money is supposed to reflect the Bahá'í principles and the Bahá'í life.

Bahá'ís are not food faddists, and they don't believe in staying away from motion pictures, night clubs, theaters, or parties. They do, however, prefer not to be part of an alcoholic atmosphere or one of degenerate entertainment and stimulation, since these are primarily a waste of time to those with worthier things to do.

Bahá'ís are expected to educate their children in the Bahá'í teachings, and to celebrate the nine Bahá'í Holy Days by staying away from school or jobs when possible. In America the Bahá'ís have acquainted many schools and innumerable employers with the dates of their Holy Days, receiving in turn a great deal of co-operation in that regard, thanks to the American belief in religious freedom.

Bahá'í marriages are legal in a majority of the states of the United States, and Bahá'í funerals—with their requirements of simplicity and a lack of rigid ceremony—are becoming increasingly popular, even when the deceased's family are not Bahá'ís.

Bahá'ís sincerely try to be modest, humble, and self-effacing. They believe that nothing they do would be possible without the assistance of Bahá'u'lláh and the Heavenly Concourse. There are many famous Bahá'ís, but seldom would one know this in Bahá'í circles, since these believers act simply and modestly with their fellow believers, and are known only through professional publicity given to their careers.

Bahá'ís do not believe in recriminations when one of the believers is rebuked administratively. When he returns to the activities, he is treated just as lovingly, and no reference is made to past misdemeanors.

Bahá'ís do not claim to be anything but human beings. They know anger, they know hurt, they have the same kinds of personal, financial, and business problems that people have who are not Bahá'ís. They feel, however, that in their teachings they have the answer to help them live through such situations more easily, and that through Bahá'í prayer they can eventually acquire the strength to live more calmly through the problems they must face each day of their lives.

The Local Spiritual Assembly

One thing that makes life simpler—and happier—for Bahá'ís is the knowledge that they always have their administrative bodies to turn to for guidance.

The Local Spiritual Assembly is a group of nine believers for whom the majority of the Bahá'ís in a community have voted as being best able to serve its needs for the coming year.

The nine newly elected Assembly members vote for their own officers: a chairman, vice-chairman, secretary (often, in a large community the secretary's functions are divided between a corresponding secretary and a recording secretary), and treasurer. These offices are only for the purposes of fulfilling certain set duties of the Assembly; in consultation all nine members have the same privileges and duty of expressing their opinion.

The fact that a believer is a member of the Local Assembly carries no authority outside of Local Assembly meetings or an assignment given to be carried out as the Assembly representative. The Bahá'ís on an Assembly are considered as having the same consultative status at Nineteen-Day Feasts as the other members of the community, except for the chairmanning of the Feast and the reading of reports by the secretary and treasurer of the Assembly. Assembly members have the same privileges in their community activities as the other members. They cannot preen themselves on an "exalted" position that does not exist individually. Only in consultation together, as an Assembly, does a divinely ordained administrative body exist, so that as individuals these Bahá'ís think for themselves, not for the community.

Over and over the emphasis is placed on Bahá'ís learning to express humility and modesty in the Bahá'í work they perform. Members of Assemblies are requested not to speak of Assembly matters outside of an Assembly meeting unless assigned to do so by the Assembly for administrative reasons. If a believer has a problem to present to the Assembly, he requests an appointment through its secretary, then discusses only that portion of his problem which he feels is pertinent to the body in making its decision or offering its suggestions.

Matters discussed at Assembly meetings remain inviolate, except for the information that may possibly be required by other administrative bodies, such as the National Assembly, for their knowledge or use.

Even the members of Bahá'í committees learn to work in groups, not as individuals. They too elect a chairman and secretary for each committee, and express only the will of the entire committee, not of individuals, nor do they discuss committee business outside of committee meetings.

Personal feelings and differences have no part in Assembly meetings or discussions. Bahá'ís try to emphasize the adjuration to look at a person's motive and to give him the benefit of any possible doubt. If a Bahá'í violates an ordinance or part of the moral code he is given one, two, even three warnings by the Assembly before the matter is finally passed on to the National Assembly along with local recommendations for its disposition. Many times the national body will accept the local body's recommendations.

It is only when an obligatory Bahá'í law has been broken that there cannot be any flexibility, since the penalties for the breaking of such laws are clearly stated and adduced.

Assembly members aim to be united in their devotion and understanding of the principles of Bahá'í Administration, and humble in their desire to serve. Such unity does not require similar personalities, that they be around the same age, or that they have compatible education or number of years in the Faith. Neither does unity mean constant and complete agreement in all matters. The fact of complete agreement is commensurate with the Assembly's unity of spirit.

Bahá'ís realize that one of the difficulties is the possible clash of differing personalities. A Bahá'í Assembly strives to solve such clashes on a spiritual basis, by facing its problems squarely. They realize that the seemingly divergent talents of Assembly members are essential to that body's work. Personalities as such do not count, since the Faith is too great for any one believer to decide to secure a petty triumph over another, and even if he did decide to try to do so, it would not be possible.

The Local Assembly is planned as the focal point to express the developing conscience of the Bahá'í community. Its members know that because the outside world remains so hopelessly divided, the Faith itself stands on trial with many of those who are not Bahá'ís. They are waiting to see whether the avowed followers of Bahá'u'lláh can rise to the highest form of moral action so as eventually to provide all mankind with the means of peace and spiritual freedom through their own example.

Nonbelievers are naturally not aware that Bahá'ís are constantly reminded that Bahá'u'lláh has laid down the precept that justice is the *first* and best-beloved of all things in His sight. An Assembly has a constant duty and opportunity to demonstrate Bahá'í justice. In their committee appointments they try objectively to select Bahá'ís who have demonstrated their abilities, and to disregard the matter of pleasing egos or individual cravings for attention. Another Bahá'í principle is that it is not possible to sacrifice the good of the whole merely to satisfy a part, and it can take great moral courage for administrative bodies to render such justice accordingly.

In handling community problems, there is again the matter of Bahá'í justice. An individual Bahá'í can forgive another Bahá'í, but an Assembly is not permitted to "forgive" anyone who has wronged the Bahá'í community. This would be tantamount to approval of a wrong action, and it is not the good of individuals or the Assembly which is involved, but that of the whole community.

The spirit of Bahá'í justice has been planned as a group spirit, not as an individual one. At no point in the administrative procedure for Bahá'ís will there be found a single line permitting an individual to dispense justice for his community. Always it is up to a group. In that way there is brought to bear the varied experiences and backgrounds, the fusing of different views, with an opportunity for the group, such as the Local Assembly, to consider impersonally and objectively the particular problem in applying Bahá'í principles to the outcome.

It is also important for a Bahá'í Assembly to both lead and encourage its community, to see that committees submit regular, factual reports, and never to forget that one of its objectives is the emphasis on local Bahá'í teaching efforts.

Each Assembly member is supposed to become well informed of conditions within the local community, to learn about the abilities and needs of the individual believers, and to emphasize through his example that the Assembly consists of devoted servants and trustees for the Faith by being as loving, kind, and helpful to his fellow Bahá'ís as he can.

The Bahá'ís believe no community is stronger than its administrative body. From that institution stems the spiritual life of the Bahá'ís as well as the direction of the activities which help to sustain all the Institutions of the Faith.

Every decision of the Local Assembly reflects on the community, regardless of the topic under discussion. The Assembly represents the spirit of the Bahá'í teachings to the believers and to those who are not of the Faith but are watching its actions and its results.

The Dawn and
the New Day

The Dawn — The Báb

WHENEVER MANKIND has been left unattended spiritually, it has seemed to fall into a general lethargy for a while. Then, as the need for guidance is stimulated once more, it bursts forth in various ways. So it was during the nineteenth century. Throughout the world, people were bursting from the shells of their inactivity. New inventions were being developed, progressive ideas were being tested, and in an instinctive search for spiritual truths, old prophecies were being renewed.

Among these prophecies was the belief that sometime between the years 1843 and 1847, His Holiness, Jesus Christ, would reappear on earth.

Should you search through the scriptures of any divinely revealed religion, you will find that God has never sent His messengers to a place having no need of them—be it a town, a city, or a country that is fairly content, progressive, or spiritually aware—it learns indirectly of God's newest affirmations. Instead, such messengers seem to arise where they are needed most, in a place where God's laws have been so amended, neglected, or trampled upon, that they have become vague memories to the populace.

This was the condition in the ancient country of Persia (now

48

called Iran) two hundred years ago. From a period of nearly unimaginable greatness and magnificence, when she had dominated the entire world of nations with her culture and achievements, by 1844 she had sunk to the lowliest condition of corruption, tyranny, and poverty.

Her Shahs were either hopelessly inept or monstrously cruel. Her clergy was bigoted and intolerant. Her people were fettered by ignorance, superstition, and suppression. Due to far too many religious divisions, men lived in fear of the slightest contact with another who believed in something different from their own beliefs. It was a time when the mere act of physically brushing against a "nonbeliever" might result in a fight to the death between the two protagonists.

The Muslim beliefs had divided men into so many religious sects warring with each other that little more than a state of decadence remained as evidence of the ancient glories. Education was neglected, sanitation had become virtually extinct, safety was a mirage and justice had vanished. Western science and art were looked upon as unclean and contrary to the approved religious beliefs. In spite of all this and the deliberate attempts to mock what Persia had once been, there were still some awakened minds and souls living there, many great scholars whom nothing could destroy. They kept alive the belief that eventually there would appear the promised one of God who, it had been prophesied, would return to earth to liberate the souls of men, and each such scholar taught others, who became their disciples, and pleaded with them to go out and seach for this promised one of God.

One scholar was the great teacher Ahmad-i-Ahsá'í. His heir to this holy search was Siyyid Kázim, who in turn so inspired his pupil Mullá Husayn that that young man believed there was nothing else as important as to travel by foot as long as was necessary, and search for the One.

Bahá'í history records:

Drawn as if by a magnet which seemed to attract him irresistibly towards the north, he proceeded to Shíráz. . . . On that very day, a few hours before sunset, whilst walking outside the gate of the city, his eyes fell suddenly upon a Youth of radiant countenance, who wore a green turban and who, advancing towards him, greeted him with a smile of loving welcome. He embraced Mullá Ḥusayn with tender affection as though he had been his intimate and lifelong friend. . . .

The Youth invited the traveler to His home to rest after the long journey and Mullá Ḥusayn, after first demurring, finally accepted, and during their conversation was most impressed by the magnetism of his Host, His gait, the charm of His voice and the dignity of His bearing.

After extending hospitality and refreshment to His visitor, the Youth sat down to talk with him, and learned of Mullá Ḥusayn's goal.

"Has your teacher," the Bahá'ís are told the Youth asked, "given you any detailed indications as to the distinguishing features of the promised One?"

"Yes," Mullá Ḥusayn answered. "He is of a pure lineage, is of illustrious descent, and of the seed of Fáṭimih. As to His age, He is more than twenty and less than thirty. He is endowed with innate knowledge. He is of medium height, abstains from smoking, and is free from bodily deficiency."

Mullá Ḥusayn's Host paused and then vibrantly declared: "Behold, all these signs are manifest in Me!"

For hours He deposed each of the signs and explained them to Mullá Ḥusayn's amazement and growing belief that his search was ended. One of these proofs was a treatise created by Mullá Ḥusayn, himself, bearing upon certain abstruse and hidden teachings he had learned. Another was to have revealed a commentary on the Súrih of Joseph in a style and language not at all like that of the times. Both of these requests were fulfilled without the slightest hesitation or error. The Súrih of Joseph was written with such incredible rapidity and accompanied by the most beautifully spoken words that it kept His listener enraptured. They continued to converse together, and, whenever Mullá Ḥusayn listened, he was spellbound and oblivious of time or anything. To him the cadences of that divine voice were the most enthralling music he had ever heard.

Finally the Host addressed His guest:

"O thou who art the first to believe in Me! Verily, I say, I am the Báb, the Gate of God, and thou art the Báhu'l-Báb, the gate of that Gate. Eighteen souls must, in the beginning, spontaneously and of their own accord, accept Me and recognize the truth of My Revelation. Unwarned and uninvited each of these must seek independently to find Me. . . ."

This was May 23, 1844. It is a date revered by all Bahá'ís of yesteryear and today as the Anniversary of the Declaration of the Báb.

When Mullá Ḥusayn left the Báb the next morning, he had promised not to tell anyone else about his great discovery. It was to remain a secret until all the other "Letters of the Living," as the first eighteen disciples were called by the Báb, had searched Him out for themselves.

After they found Him, the next stage began of His ministry of love, fear, and truth, a twofold mission that was destined to last only nine years.

The world would eventually learn that the Báb was Himself not only an independent Manifestation of God, but dually was also the Herald of One greater than Himself, to Whom He referred as "Him Whom God Shall Make Manifest."

In turn, the One to follow the Báb would be the Inaugurator of a new and unprecedented era in the religious history of mankind, as Bahá'í records would note.

The Bahá'ís earnestly believe that the claim to the twofold station ordained for the Báb by God constitutes one of the most distinctive features of the Bahá'í Revelation. It is a further evidence to them of the uniqueness, mysterious power, and authority with which the Bahá'í holy cycle has been invested. The Báb's

Revelation, in fact, was so fraught with significance and purpose that it set into motion events which have forever changed the pattern of future civilizations.

Until His twenty-fifth year on earth the Báb had been known as Siyyid 'Alí Muḥammad, son of a merchant who had died when He was very young. As a little boy He had been primarily reared by His uncle. Siyyid is the title given in Islámic circles to those who are the acknowledged descendants of the Prophet Muḥammad, entitling them to wear a green turban as their mark of illustrious descent.

Even as a child, the Báb was remarkable for His innate knowledge, although only His schoolteacher seemed to recognize this unique quality. When His tutor confessed that he was unable to teach the young boy anything, the Báb's uncle released his nephew from all formal instruction. Always, the Báb knew things that never came from books, but people in those days were not easily impressed by outer signs of wisdom and understood little about divine prophets who might be living under their own gaze.

At the age of twenty-two, He married a young cousin. Their tiny son died at the age of one year, and by 1844 'Alí Muḥammad was known to His family and friends as a remarkably pious, wise, and noble young man of unusually fine character. Outwardly He had no problems. His life appeared perfect to those around Him, and He seemed destined for the routinely pleasant existence of the well-to-do class into which He had been born and raised.

How could anyone sense or know that His mind was on far more serious, spiritual things than what concerned the average person? How could they suspect that He was girding His heart and soul for the heroic efforts of those in the service of God? How could they guess that His entire life must have led up to the moment of His Declaration to Mullá Ḥusayn that momentous date of May 23, 1844?

It took another forty days after May 23 before the enrollment occurred of even the first of the remaining seventeen Letters of the Living. Why these companions of His soul and suffering were called this has not been made clear, but to Bahá'ís they were obviously destined of God to help and support the Báb in His first phases of His ministry on earth.

Shoghi Effendi, the late Guardian of the Faith, has given this description:

". . . Gradually, spontaneously, some in sleep, others while awake, some through fasting and prayer, others through dreams and visions, they discovered the Object of their quest. . . . The last, but in rank the first . . . was the erudite, the twenty-two-year-old Quddús. . . . Immediately preceding him, a woman, the only one of her sex who, unlike her fellow disciples, never attained the presence of the Báb. . . . A poetess, less than thirty years of age, of distinguished birth, of bewitching charm, of captivating eloquence, indomitable in spirit, unorthodox in her views, audacious in her acts, immortalized as Ṭáhirih (the Pure One) . . . had, in consequence of the appearance of the Báb to her in a dream, received the first intimation of (His) Cause. . . ."

As soon as all eighteen Letters of the Living were assembled, they were sent by the Báb to various parts of the land, enjoining each to a specific task in the spreading of the new Faith.

These new teachings of justice and mercy and love and forgiveness, equality and liberty, aroused the admiration of those hungry for them, but increased the alarm of the rulers of Persia, inciting them to rage. There commenced a series of imprisonments, deportations, examinations before the tribunals, scourgings, indignities, and torments that often defied description. All of the Báb's Letters of the Living were martyred for carrying His Message to the people.

His followers were also martyred, in the most abominable ways imaginable—beheaded, hanged, blown from the mouths of cannon, burned, or chopped to pieces. But just as in the days of Christ, nothing could stop the Word of God from spreading. Many of the Báb's followers were encouraged by the fact that the martyrdoms and terror seemed to be a fulfillment of the prophecies concerning His Coming. One was translated from the writings of the Shi'ih sect of Islam:

"In Him shall be the perfection of Moses, the preciousness of Jesus, and the patience of Job; His saints shall be abased in His time, and their heads shall be exchanged as presents . . . the earth shall be dyed with their blood and lamentation shall prevail amongst their women; these are My saints indeed."

The Life of the Báb resembles greatly the life of each divine prophet preceding Him, especially that of the Christ. The Báb has been described as "gentle, irresistible, matchless in His meekness, imperturbable in His serenity, magnetic in His utterance, and unrivaled in the dramatic episodes of His swift and tragic ministry."

Much of the enmity against Him was because He would not content Himself with merely declaring His Mission, but insisted on following this with action and great exhortation, as described in part by Shoghi Effendi:

The implications of a Revelation thrust so dramatically upon a race so degenerate . . . could indeed have had no other consequence. . . . A Faith whose Founder . . . regarded Himself as the precursor of One incomparably greater than Himself, who peremptorily commanded not only the subjects of the Sháh, but the monarch himself, and even the kings and princes of the earth, to forsake their all and follow Him, who claimed to be the inheritor of the earth and all that is therein—a Faith Whose religious doctrines, Whose ethical standards, social principles, and religious laws challenged the whole structure of the society in which it was born, soon ranged, with startling unanimity, the mass of the people behind their priests, and behind their chief magistrate, with his ministers and his government, and welded them into an opposition sworn to destroy, root and branch, the movement initiated by One Whom they regarded as an impious and presumptuous pretender.

Each episode in the Báb's life can be compared to similar ones in the lives of the preceding manifestations of God. There have already been written many Bahá'í volumes detailing the steps of

the Báb's persecution, His exile and His imprisonment. His chal-
lenging world mission was a symbol of the Oneness of the
Prophets. His call to regeneration of character and renewal of
faith and to the teachings of unity have become a clarion call that
has reechoed since His Declaration.

Consider the Báb on the momentous and horrifying occasion
at the marketplace of Tabríz where He gave up His life. Then
think of Moses' forty years in the wilderness, the burden he bore,
Moses, the Law-giver. You might stand at the foot of the Cross
and hear the cries of the rabble casting lots for the clothing of
Christ, a lordly king. You might even accompany Muḥammad,
the prophet of Arabia whose flight to Medina from Mecca nevertheless presaged an Age of Glory.

Or, you might picture the morning of July 9, 1850, when Sám
Khán, an Armenian who hated confessing to the Báb that it was
his duty to order the shots for His execution and, as someone
who now also believed in the Báb, asked what he could do. The
Báb asked him to pray and advised that if the prayer was sincere
it would be answered.

Imagine how surprised the guard must have been who came
to the Báb's cell for a praying Man, and instead found Him
giving instructions to a follower. The Báb announced sweetly
that He was not ready to leave, but His words were ignored. He
was taken away, and trussed up with ropes and tied to a great
iron ring that had been set in the wall of the prison square.
Trussed across His breast was a young disciple who had pleaded
to be allowed to die with His Beloved.

Right to the last minute Sám Khán waited, and when it was
obvious that no answer was forthcoming to his prayers he had to
order the shots to be fired. Two hundred and fifty sharpshooters
were prone, two hundred and fifty knelt, and two hundred and
fifty stood. It would seem impossible for at least some of their
bullets not to hit the mark, but when the smoke of the firing
cleared away, the Báb was nowhere in sight, the ropes were all

that had been hit and the young disciple stood alone, dazed and uninjured.

In the prison the guards found the Báb once more in His cell, calmly finishing His words to His follower.

Sám Khán, ashen-faced and trembling, went to the governor of the prison and refused to continue the horrendous assignment. "It is a miracle from God and my men will not shoot Him," he declared.

At noon a new company of sharpshooters were ready. This time the Báb went willingly to His execution. When the smoke cleared away, the bodies of the Báb and the young believer had been completely riddled by the bullets, but their faces had scarcely been touched!

The bodies were thrown over the prison wall into a moat. Later they were found and taken away by some of the Báb's followers, and for fifty years remained hidden in various places, the believers afraid the precious remains might be desecrated or destroyed by the enemies of the Faith. At the end of that period, 'Abdu'l-Bahá brought them to Mount Carmel for burial.

Later Shoghi Effendi raised the beautiful golden-domed tomb on the side of Mount Carmel that has become a landmark to all who visit Haifa, Israel.

The New Day — Bahá'u'lláh

THE MARTYRDOM of the Báb left His followers so bereft of guidance that they might have fulfilled the Sháh's base wishes and become scattered to the winds, the Faith forgotten, except that God had willed otherwise.

One follower was a young nobleman, Mírzá Husayn 'Alí, Prince of Nur. He worked night and day to restore their flagging spirits and to encourage their continued efforts. He was so successful that again the Sháh became enraged at his failure to completely exterminate this new Faith. One day while he was out riding his horse, two young boys shot at him but missed. It didn't matter that he never found out whether they did it from religious fervor or as a youthful prank. This was enough of an excuse for another bloody campaign against the Báb's followers.

This time Husayn-'Alí was among the new captives thrown into prison. The dungeon was a dark, damp place known as the Síyáh-Chál, which means the Black Hole. Its walls were never dry. No light ever entered. The one hundred and fifty prisoners there were squeezed tightly together. Over their shoulders was cast a heavy iron chain with an iron collar for each neck.

To each prophet of God there has come the specific moment of revelation when he personally knew—or was told in some way—who he was and his station on earth. To Christ it came when the dove descended upon him as he stood in the River Jordan. To Zoroaster it came in a series of seven visions with the Angel Gabriel, and it was this same Angel Gabriel who came to Muhammad in the Cave.

Husayn-'Alí had all His life been used to comfort, even luxury. You can imagine him down in that Black Hole trying to help the other prisoners, never able to forget for a moment why all of them were there and yet never regretting the reason, either. This has been the way with all religious martyrs. They have sought death for their beliefs as a thirsty man seeks the riverbank, to wash away the memory of their sufferings and to know that they did it for the One True God Who had sent down still another Message for His unhappy people.

One night in that horrible hole of blackness a heavenly Angel appeared in a vision to Husayn-'Alí. This Angel told Him in words of great beauty Who He was, the Glory of God upon this earth, meant to point out to mankind the way it could achieve the Kingdom of God upon earth. The Truth became real to Him and He accepted what He knew was to be His earthly burden. He felt Himself able to bear the suffering that had been forced upon each of God's prophets because He was God's Appointed.

Seldom before had a divine prophet also been a prince of the realm, even though He became a Prince of Heaven. Husayn-'Alí was henceforth to be known as Bahá'u'lláh (The Glory and Splendor of God).

Bahá'u'lláh's father owned many palaces and was looked up to by his contemporaries for both his wealth and his genius. Bahá-'u'lláh was born in 1817 and it is said that His parents had a special love for Him, despite their having other children. Even in His infancy He seemed to radiate and display remarkable power.

Bahá'u'lláh did not have, nor did He need, any formal schooling as a child. Like the Báb, even as a youngster He was possessed of innate knowledge.

When His mother said, ". . . He is very bright," His father replied, "But you do not know what a glorious soul is in His body," showing that Bahá'u'lláh's father may have sensed His Son's future as the Chosen One of God.

The Báb's future signs of Prophethood and His uniqueness were not generally recognized. From almost the start of Bahá-'u'lláh's life, however, people prophesied that He would be a great and wise Man. It is said He was so beloved by all that even His father's enemies withheld their attacks because of Him.

At the time His father died, Bahá'u'lláh had the reputation of being the wisest, most spiritual Person in the province. He was called upon whenever anyone needed guidance or help. At the time of the Báb's Declaration, Bahá'u'lláh was twenty-six years old. To those who asked what He thought of the Báb's Declaration, He answered:

"What the Báb says is true."

The Báb is known to have written to Bahá'u'lláh at least once, so it is believed that their spiritual communication was strong and constant.

After the Báb's martyrdom Bahá'u'lláh traveled to Karbilá and Baghdád to help and inspire many of the Báb'ís through His own example and knowledge.

He could have avoided the Sháh's persecution, had He so desired. The Prime Minister had sent Him a warning message a short time before Bahá'u'lláh was captured with the other be-

lievers, begging Him to depart from the city and save Himself.
Bahá'u'lláh refused, and shortly after, a mob arrived at His palace,
compelling Him to run for miles with manacled hands, and
barefoot, while they jeered at Him.

Bahá'u'lláh remained in the Black Hole for four months. Each
day a different follower of the new Faith was taken out to be
martyred in the public square. In spite of the depression they
should have felt, the remaining prisoners were cheered and up-
lifted because of Bahá'u'lláh's Presence. Comforted by Him, they
sang and their chanting became so loudly exultant that it could
be heard in the Sháh's palace, to the despot's great annoyance.

Bahá'u'lláh would chant, "God is Our Sustainer," "Sufficient
unto Us is God," and there would be unlimited joy felt within
that otherwise comfortless dungeon. It is said that in their renunciation and spiritual excitement, condemned prisoners sang
and danced, even under the swords of their executioners. They
found a glory in their spiritual sacrifice that can only be understood by others who have continued to believe in their God under
great duress, the true believers of any religion who become on
fire with their Faith.

Meanwhile, the persistent and decisive intervention of the influential Russian Ambassador, among others interceding, resulted
in Bahá'u'lláh's release at last from the Black Hole.

His freedom was of short duration. He had barely rejoined His
family when the Sháh ordered Him to leave Persia within a
month. The only softening of this harsh decree was that Bahá-
'u'lláh could personally choose the place to which He would be
exiled.

The Russian friend offered Him the protection of his own
government, and every possible facility for moving to and living
in Russia, but Bahá'u'lláh, thanking him earnestly, decided on
Baghdád instead.

Shoghi Effendi explained this:

> The Sháh's edict, equivalent to an order for the immediate
> expulsion of Bahá'u'lláh . . . will even be recognized to have

ushered in one of the most eventful and momentous epochs in the world's religious history. It coincides with the inauguration of a ministry extending over a period of almost forty years—a ministry which, by virtue of its creative power, its cleansing force, its healing influences, and the irresistible operation of the world-directing, world-shaping forces it released, stands unparalleled in the religious annals of the entire human race. . . .

However, at that time, it sounded to most of His followers like nothing short of disaster. There was no time for Him to obtain money or even the clothing necessary for Himself and those who accompanied Him, since the government had confiscated all His wealth and possessions. The hardships were unimaginable as they rode on their horses over perilous mountain roads. They were escorted by an officer of the Imperial Bodyguard and an official of the Russian Legation, apparently because Bahá'u'lláh's influential Russian friend was still concerned about His welfare.

Arriving in Baghdád, Bahá'u'lláh found the Báb'ís there completely demoralized. Just having Bahá'u'lláh in their midst was stimulating. He determined to set them an Example to Whom they could turn for guidance, to elevate their characters, reform their deeds, and transform their weaknesses into strength and uprightness.

Within a short time the group's weakness became power, its inharmony had turned into unity, the evil habits into good deeds. Spurred on by the special glow they acquired, new followers joined those already in Baghdád.

Naturally this did not change the hearts of those who felt Bahá'u'lláh had taken over where they had failed. They resented His natural leadership and insisted He was usurping their rightful place.

Bahá'u'lláh had not even declared His own Mission or Station. There was no basis for jealous, personal attacks on Him, but the very fact that He became so beloved by others within a short time was enough reason for those intent upon evil deeds and thoughts.

Without telling anyone of His plans, one night Bahá'u'lláh left. Nobody knew where He had gone. He took with Him nothing but a dervísh's bowl (a mark of material detachment) and a change of clothes, and traveled until He reached the wilderness area where He lived in a shelter on top of a mountain and then alone in a cave.

He sought out no one. The area was known to be filled with highwaymen and other desperadoes, but at night when His melodious voice could be heard chanting exquisite Persian prayers and poems from the cave, whoever could hear Him tiptoed nearer to listen to the wonderful singing. Forgotten were their own evil deeds or plans. They knew nothing about Who Bahá'u'lláh really was, but still He filled them with love and admiration for His spiritual qualities.

Soon their children came to Him for help with their school work. It was because of one such child who showed Bahá'u'lláh's fine penmanship to his teacher that word eventually spread about a learned man who lived in a cave. This news finally spread as far as Baghdád, from where the believers sent an emissary on the long, hard journey, begging Bahá'u'lláh to return to them.

At first He refused. Not until the delegate showed Him the many letters that were filled with promises and stories of their need of Him did Bahá'u'lláh relent and return to them.

This time things were better. For seven years love blossomed among the Báb'ís and there was great progress in the spreading of the Báb's teachings. Even the Kurdistán people came down from the mountains to be with the Wise One, and a new spirit of love and unity shone in Baghdád. More and more followers were drawn to the new Faith and farther and farther did the stories go about Bahá'u'lláh's work among the people.

Every street near His house became thronged with those who visited Him from all over. He taught them that the way to spread the Báb's teachings was for each person to become a divine lamp of guidance. The more they were persecuted for their beliefs, the more they would have to demonstrate love and kindness, not only to their friends but to their enemies.

It was well that He gave them such guidance. They were to need it. Soon after, a friend warned Bahá'u'lláh of still another plot by His powerful Persian government enemies. With Divine Knowledge, He nodded and replied calmly:

"God is working through invisible means."

In many of the Bahá'í Holy Books it is said that the Faith will suffer persecution in order to spread. Not only then, even for today. So it proved from those earliest beginnings. The small group of Báb'ís in Baghdád grew to many times that number after Bahá'u'lláh's return to them and during the seven quiet years of study. Bahá'u'lláh had still not told them of His true Station. Their beliefs gradually took shape and Bahá'u'lláh still spoke and acted as one of the foremost disciples of the Báb and still taught in the Báb's Name.

A distinguishing feature of the Bahá'í Faith is the fact that the Founder, Bahá'u'lláh, personally took pen in hand, and wrote "The Hidden Words" and many other immortal works still extant. Moreover, His Writings were more voluminous than those set down by the companions of Jesus, Muhammad, and the other Holy Messengers. The purity of the Bahá'í Scriptures is incontestable because these revelations were recorded by Bahá'u'ulláh or through a secretary to whom He dictated and whose transcription He personally corrected or approved.

One example of His productive flow is that when He walked in a garden He dictated so rapidly that the secretary had to take it down quickly in some kind of contrived shorthand. Thoughts, ideas, and words came instinctively to Bahá'u'lláh. He didn't plan them, prepare them in advance or have notes. They were simply the outpourings of the Divine Will of God through Bahá'u'ulláh's mouth or pen.

Bahá'u'lláh's Writings, as well as those of 'Abdu'l-Bahá and Shoghi Effendi, His Interpreters, demonstrate the manner in which Bahá'u'lláh was the clear Channel through Whom God, the Unknowable, chooses to be known, since God's only Channel is a prophet or Manifestation of God. Unfortunately, many of His revealed prayers were completely lost, as they were taken down mainly when people listening to Him remembered to record His chants.

He wrote many of His Tablets, however, in His own handwriting, and His script was steady and firm until the time later when He was poisoned in Adrianople. From that time on His handwriting was shaky.

In both His Writings and His words to the followers, Bahá'-u'lláh emphasized cleanliness. Nothing of the dust should blow in anywhere. Each person's dress and costume must be spotless. If not, one's prayers would never reach God. However, He made certain to explain that God would forgive those who did not follow this, if they had good reasons.

Many of the Báb's Tablets have been lost, also. The Persian government had announced that if anything written by Him were found in anyone's house, that house would be leveled to the ground.

As the year of 1863 drew closer, Bahá'u'lláh worked harder and harder, especially at His writing. Many festive Odes and Tablets poured forth from Him, and often His companions spent a whole night singing and chanting them. The number of His verses was no more remarkable either, than the wealth and diversity of subjects to which they referred.

"The undeniable evidences of the range and magnificence of Bahá'u'lláh's rising power; His rapidly waxing prestige; the miraculous transformation which, by precept and example He had effected in the outlook and character of His companions from Baghdád to the remotest towns and hamlets in Persia; the consuming love for Him that glowed in their bosoms," Shoghi Effendi has written, ". . . a spark was all that was required to ignite this combustible material of all the accumulated hatreds, fears, and jealousies which the revived activities of the Bábís had inspired. . . ."

At first Bahá'u'lláh's enemies tried to lie about Him so that

He would be extradited in disgrace to Persia, but this failed. Then they created more lies and false instances to arouse the populace against Him, but these efforts also failed. Even when meeting face to face with His enemies on the street, Bahá'u'lláh never flinched. He would let them know exactly what they were trying to do, and they would be so abashed and confused they would be forced to abandon whatever current mischief had been their intent.

"The consul-general," Shoghi Effendi explains, "had even gone so far as to hire a ruffian, a Turk . . . for the sum of one hundred tumans, [to] provide him with a horse and with two pistols, and order him to seek out and kill Bahá'u'lláh. . . . [He] eluded the vigilance of the Bábís [and] entered the bath with a pistol concealed in his cloak . . . only to discover that he lacked the courage to accomplish his task."

Another time the same would-be assassin tried lying in wait for Bahá'u'lláh with a gun. Once again he was so frightened that the shooting iron dropped from his grasp. Bahá'u'lláh picked it up and returned it, then had His own escort accompany the fear-stricken villain back to his residence.

Other plots were tried and failed, but it was obvious that the years of uninterrupted, patient, and successful work in Baghdád and nearby terrains were drawing to a close. Bahá'í historians point out that again and again Bahá'u'lláh referred to an approaching period of trial and turmoil for the believers, His mien so sad that it disturbed His closest associates.

One Tablet of Bahá'u'lláh told of a dream He had:

> I saw the prophets and the messengers gather and seat themselves around Me, moaning, weeping, and loudly lamenting. Amazed, I inquired of them the reason, whereupon their lamentations and weeping waxed greater, and they said unto me: "We weep for Thee, O Most Great Mystery, O Tabernacle of Immortality!" They wept with such a weeping that I too wept with them. Thereupon the Concourse on high addressed me saying: ". . . Erelong shalt Thou behold with Thine own eyes what no prophet hath beheld. . . . Be patient, be patient." . . .

They continued addressing Me the whole night until the approach of dawn.

Shortly thereafter Bahá'u'lláh received a courteous invitation to proceed as a Guest of the Ottoman government to Constantinople. They offered Him a mounted escort for His protection and Bahá'u'lláh accepted.

On April 22, 1863, thirty-one days after the Bábí New Year, Bahá'u'lláh set forth on the first stage of the four months' journey destined to end in Constantinople, the capital of the Ottoman Empire. Since then, the day has become historic in the Bahá'í Era and has been known as the First Day of their Riḍván Festival.

Bahá'u'lláh's followers wept and wailed as He left Baghdád, blocking His path along the route, even outside the gate. They threw themselves at His feet, stood on rooftops and crowded Him and His entourage along the way, begging that He not desert them. Nevertheless, the group finally got under way and were at last able to proceed to the place known since then to Bahá'ís as The Garden of Riḍván, where He was to wait for preparations to be made for the rest of the journey. This date was to be eventually recognized as the beginning of the holiest and most significant of all Bahá'í Festivals. It was to inaugurate the initial Declaration of His Mission for the believers only, and would be followed much later with a Declaration to the world and its rulers.

Now, at last, those who had followed the Báb so faithfully, and come into the Faith believing in the Báb's legacy, were told that in Bahá'u'lláh they had the One to Whom the Báb had referred, Whose Advent the Báb had so fervently prophesied. No longer would they call themselves Bábís. From then on they would be known as Bahá'ís, meaning the Followers of The Glory, He Who was called Bahá'u'lláh.

Shoghi Effendi explains that there was little recorded about the exact circumstances attending that first Declaration.

"The words Bahá'u'lláh actually uttered on that occasion, the

manner of His Declaration, the reaction it produced, its impact
. . . , the identity of those who were privileged to hear Him, are
shrouded in an obscurity which future historians will find it
difficult to penetrate. . . ."

On May 3, 1863, at noon, Bahá'u'lláh left the Garden of
Riḍván amid more scenes of tumultuous enthusiasm which were
noted as "no less spectacular, and even more touching than those
which greeted Him when leaving His . . . House in Baghdád. . . ."

Mounted on a red roan stallion, He rode forth attracting
mighty waves of love and greeting and loyalty, such as even a
King of Kings might expect to attract. He was accompanied by
His family and twenty-six of His disciples. Also, fifty mules, a
mounted guard of ten officers, and other signs of honor were
included in the equipment. Delegations awaited to cheer Him
at each stop with lavish feasts and proofs of admiration and
devotion that His enemies had never counted upon when hoping
He would exit in disgrace from Baghdád.

The arrival at Constantinople developed into, as Shoghi Effendi describes it, "the grimmest and most calamitous and yet the
most glorious chapter in the history of the first Bahá'í century. . . ."

It was a period in which the gravest privations and trials would
be mingled with the noblest of spiritual triumph. It took only
four months for the intrigues of Bahá'u'lláh's enemies from the
Persian court to do their work. Bahá'u'lláh referred to Constantinople (Istanbul) as the "throne of tyranny" and consistently refused ot pay courtesy calls on the tyrant's lackeys,
the political and religious authorities, no matter how highly
placed, or even to return the calls paid Him by several ministers.
They looked only at what they called His faults, and they
punished Him in a manner planned to make His worst enemies
become their happiest.

The Sultan, self-styled vicar and absolute ruler of the mighty
empire, banished Bahá'u'lláh and His whole entourage. It was
in the depth of winter and Bahá'u'lláh was not asked this time
where He might like to go. He and His group were sent to

Adrianople under the most degrading and humiliating circumstances, a city so far away that it was situated on the farthest edge of the empire.

For the third time Bahá'u'lláh, His family and their companions went into exile. This time they departed ignominiously. Some of them rode in wagons, others on pack animals, their belongings piled into carts drawn by oxen. They set out on a cold December morning accompanied by harsh Turkish officers. It took twelve days to traverse that bleak and windswept country in order to reach Adrianople. This was the city which Bahá'u'lláh Himself has described as "the place which none entereth except such as have rebelled against the authority of the sovereign. . . . Neither My family, nor those who accompanied Me had the necessary raiment to protect them from the . . . freezing weather. . . . The eyes of Our enemies wept over Us and . . . those of every discerning person. . . ."

The dwelling to which they were assigned for that first week was actually meant only for summer habitation. Not until six months later were they moved to quarters that were fairly comfortable. It was so dreary that little did anyone realize how famous it would become as the setting for the most glorious spiritual phase of the Bahá'í Era.

The Most Great Prisoner

NO AMOUNT of torment, deprivation, or change could interfere with the work Bahá'u'lláh knew He must do. He was determined to create His Tablets to the leaders of the world so that each and every one of them would know what could happen to those who would thwart God's purposes. Despite His enemies, whose onslaughts seemed to grow strong with time, Bahá'u'lláh conducted Himself and led His followers with such dignity, courage, and independence that He soon won over many of the notables and people of this prison city. It only created more hatred, of course, from those far away who wished Him ill.

Desperate attempts were made upon His life and those of His companions. An attempt to poison Bahá'u'lláh happened when He accepted an invitation to tea in the home of someone pretending to be a friend. He was felled by the poisonous substance smeared upon the lip of His cup, and had an illness of a month's duration accompanied by severe pains and high fever. Never again would His Writings be strong and flow easily. His palsied hand would produce only shaky writing for the rest of His life.

Another murderous attempt was made on Him when the water in a well used by His family and companions was also poisoned, but it made them only slightly ill. An attempt was made to bribe Bahá'u'lláh's barber to kill Him, but the barber instead advised Bahá'u'lláh of the awful plot. Lies, false documents, all kinds of other plots against Him followed. Nothing worked, but they naturally weakened His position with the country's ruling personages because of the false stories continually spread by the Persian courtiers.

And still Bahá'u'lláh continued His work, seeming to ignore the constant threat and danger to His freedom from the various forms of intrigue or violence being concentrated upon Him.

Finally there appeared the climax to all His efforts. These were His Tablets, His Directives, that ever so weighty Proclamation: His Writings to the kings of the earth, Muslim and Christian alike, to ministers and ambassadors, to the presidents and heads of the republics in the Americas, to the ecclesiastical heads of Islám, to the Vatican, to the wise men and the inhabitants of Constantinople, and to the philosophers of the world. Last, to the people of Persia, affirming that even though they put Him to death God would assuredly raise up another divine prophet in His stead! Nothing could have been so fiery, so determined, and so definitely certain to raise the increased anger and vengefulness of His enemies.

He told about the purpose and character of His Mission on earth and begged the kings to embrace His Message. He told them that the Báb's Revelation too was valid, and reproved them for ignoring what He and the Báb had brought. He begged them to become peaceful with one another and warned that "Divine chastisement" would "assail them" "from every direction" if they turned a deaf ear to what He was saying, and prophesied that even if all the doors of their kingdoms were closed to Him His Mission would still be accomplished.

He wrote separately to the various ministers of Persia and other countries who had plotted against Him, assuring that He harbored no ill-will against anyone but asking them to recognize His Mission and listen no further to lies and distortions.

He denounced the ecclesiastic leaders of Constantinople as heedless and spiritually dead, reproached them for shunning Him, detailed the full glory of the meaning of His Mission and condemned them as "worshipers of names" and "lovers of leadership."

The concluding passages were to the wise men of Constantinople and the philosophers of the world, begging them not to show pride before God, rebuking them for refusing to believe Him or to learn from Him, telling them to live righteously and with Faith and exhorting them not to "overstep the bounds of God" by turning toward man's ways and attitudes. He told the inhabitants of Constantinople that His whole gaze was for God, He could fear no one but God, that there seemed to be no one in that city wise enough to acquire the same truths that God had bestowed upon Him. He offered them the chance to listen to God, live in God's Way and turn only to God, just as He reminded the people of Persia that no matter how much they hated Him, nothing could stop Him or One after Him from proclaiming what God wished.

At first His enemies were frightened; then it brought bluster from them or those they influenced. Because they could not revenge themselves personally upon Bahá'u'lláh, now out of their reach, they turned to His followers in various countries. Once more adherents of the new Faith were imprisoned, vilified, penalized, tortured, or put to death. How Jesus Christ himself, accompanied by the Heavenly Concourse, must have seen echoed in this series of persecutions all the tribulations poured upon Him and upon every other divine messenger who tries to bring God's Message to an ailing, decaying world.

Finally Bahá'u'lláh's enemies convinced the authorities where Bahá'u'lláh was exiled, who had become incensed at the esteem shown Him by the people and the challenges of His recent Tablets and, of course, were starting to worry about His effect upon the populace itself. They decided to take immediate drastic action to annihilate the Faith, isolate its Author, and reduce His reputation to shreds. They announced His banishment to the penal colony of 'Akká.

'Akká, today known as Acre, but the original spelling will be kept here, is in Israel, which was formerly part of Syria, 'Akká, called the Most Great Prison, had a reputation of non-existent sanitation and of stench and filth. It was said that birds flying overhead dropped dead from the fumes. The plan of Bahá'u'lláh's enemies became instantly obvious, but He never protested; He submitted calmly to what He knew was God's way of bringing the new Faith to the eyes and ears of others.

The Persian Ambassador promptly informed the Persian consuls in Iraq and Egypt that the Turkish government had withdrawn its protection from the Bahá'ís, and they were free to treat all believers as they pleased. One can imagine the unspeakable cruelty and inhumanity that followed.

For five years Bahá'u'lláh's great Presence and Influence had been felt by the people of Adrianople, just as in Baghdád and Constantinople. They ignored the whisperings started by lackeys of the Prophet's enemies. They loved Bahá'u'lláh and wept openly at His departure, but there was nothing they could do to keep Him there.

He left on August 12, 1863, with His Household of family

and followers, as before. It took them twenty-two days to reach the Holy Land from Gallipoli, and the journey was difficult. The ship was small, with few means of comfort for the exiles, since whatever they brought with them was appropriated by the guards and soldiers who accompanied them.

Bahá'u'lláh's eldest Son, 'Abdu'l-Bahá, was always His comfort and joy and had recognized His Father's Divine Station while still a child. 'Abdu'l-Bahá's younger brother was called the Purest Branch, and was loved by all.

From Haifa, the group was taken by sailing boats to 'Akká, which was guarded in those days by two entrances, a land gate and a sea gate. Bahá'u'lláh remained in this Most Great Prison for two years, two months, and five days, confined to one room by Himself, while His Family had the next two rooms. The seventy companions who accompanied them in their travail, whose sole joy was to share the imprisonment of their Lord, were thrust into dungeons already filled with murderers, robbers, and outlaws.

The constant wailings, the epithets and ravings of the non-Bahá'í maddened prisoners, the cruelty of the guards, the horrible food, the crowded conditions, the stagnant air which made normal sleep impossible were all intended to weaken and demoralize the strongest of prisoners; but the believers were sustained by their love for Bahá'u'lláh and His teaching, which made everything else unimportant and easily borne.

Gradually the guards found themselves permitting some freedom to 'Abdu'l-Bahá—very little, but in comparison to the general lack of freedom the others had, it seemed great. They allowed Him to be alone for a little while each evening and to go to the morgue to meditate. Or, they would let Him stretch His legs by taking short walks to the roof with His brother, the Purest Branch, who had also won them over with his pure spirit and loving ways, even during their cruelest teasing.

The people who had traveled many miles from other cities to try to see Bahá'u'lláh in this latest imprisonment would climb on the walls of the city to catch a glimpse of Him. He would stand at His cell window and wave His hand, hoping these devoted ones would see this Sign of His love and understanding. Often the Holy Family wept together because of the sacrifice of the many who had traveled there by foot and were not granted the slightest moment with their Beloved.

Every evening the Purest Branch would go up on the roof to pray. One such evening He went to Bahá'u'lláh to ask whether His Father needed anything done for Him, since the Purest Branch had been acting in the capacity of amanuensis at times.

Bahá'u'lláh smiled and said, "Not tonight."

The Purest Branch climbed to the roof and a short while later fell through an unguarded skylight. He crashed onto a wooden crate standing on the floor beneath the skylight and it pierced his ribs.

When Bahá'u'lláh went to where the Purest Branch had been taken, He asked if His son wanted to be made whole again.

"No," was the reply.

After twenty-four hours of sheer agony which he welcomed as little enough price if it would cause Bahá'u'lláh's eventual freedom, the Purest Branch died.

The Turkish Governor started an investigation and after a few months allowed Bahá'u'lláh to leave the prison quarters to live in a small house, called "The House of Abbood," in a part of the city where the populace lived. Technically Bahá'u'lláh was still a prisoner. His freedom was limited to the area of His residence.

The inn near Abbood's House allowed two rooms to be rented for Bahá'í pilgrims who could now visit their Beloved, and the door of the land gate was opened so they could make their way more easily to Him.

It was at this time that 'Abdu'l-Bahá's tender love for Bahá'u'lláh, His concern for His Father's welfare, came to the fore. While Bahá'u'lláh concentrated on His Writing, 'Abdu'l-Bahá took charge of all other matters with such care that His loving

kindness to everyone eventually earned for Him the sobriquet of
the Exemplar and the Master to all of the Faithful.

At first the owner of the House of Abbood was afraid of
having Bahá'ís for tenants. Because of 'Abdu'l-Bahá he gradually
realized what good people they were, how spiritually inclined
were their deeds and their thoughts. When he heard that 'Abdu'l-
Bahá would be marrying a young woman who was traveling
there, he hastened to prepare a small room for the couple, in
which the ceremony would be held, and then had a second house
he owned connected with the first by a special bridge. Thus, there
was a separate apartment for 'Abdu'l-Bahá and His bride, one
for the visiting pilgrims, and the apartment occupied by Bahá'u'-
lláh.

'Abdu'l-Bahá suffered from many upper respiratory infections
and minor illnesses, but always remained kind and good-natured.
He had a wonderful sense of humor that carried the entire
household through various trying experiences, many of which
still cropped up despite the comparative freedom in which they
now lived. 'Abdu'l-Bahá desired to anticipate whatever His Father
needed, so that Bahá'u'lláh could concentrate on His work and
the other responsibilities involved in setting up the tenets for this
new Faith.

They remained at Abbood's House for seven years. During
this time Bahá'u'lláh wrote many of the most important laws
for the believers.

One day the Blessed Beauty or Ancient Beauty as Bahá'u'-
lláh also was called by the believers, said to His Son:

"Do you know it is over nine years since I have seen even a
blade of grass?"

'Abdu'l-Bahá immediately searched and found a garden that
He named "The Ridván Gardens" in memory of the original
place in Baghdàd. It is still beautiful, with its century-old pines.
When all was ready, He told His Father, but Bahá'u'lláh

refused to leave the area to which He was consigned, insisting He was still a Prisoner in 'Akká.

'Abdu'l-Bahá replied that He was imprisoning Himself and *must* come. At last, Bahá'u'lláh agreed.

Once His Father was safe at the Gardens, 'Abdu'l-Bahá rented another house with five rooms in the Mazra'ih District for all the household except Himself, His mother, and His sister.

Then He went to the owner of a house a few miles away in Bahjí and said He would like to rent it for the growing household. The owner offered it to Him without charge, saying there had been epidemics there and he didn't want to go near the place, but 'Abdu'l-Bahá insisted on paying a rental for it and later purchased the dwelling outright.

At last the Bahá'ís from Persia, Iraq, India, Egypt, and other nearby places could visit their Lord of Hosts and His Son without interference. 'Abdu'l-Bahá felt He should not live with Bahá'u'lláh even though He was the apple of His Father's eye. When He brought pilgrims to visit Bahá'u'lláh, first He would stop with them at a tea house on the end of the road, where they could wash and refresh themselves before experiencing the bounty and fulfillment of their visit with their Beloved. Eventually this tea house was called "The Tea House of the Master."

Because of 'Abdu'l-Bahá's many kindnesses to the people living in 'Akká it was He who had influenced the mayor to lift the technical boundaries of the Holy imprisonment. By the time 'Abdu'l-Bahá followed the instructions of Bahá'u'lláh to secure lands for the Faith on the side of Mount Carmel in Haifa, they were all entirely free to travel wherever they wished throughout Israel. Bahá'u'lláh had visited the site in Mount Carmel before advising His Companion, 'Abdu'l-Bahá, to try to purchase it for the Faith.

The mansion at Bahjí had actually been completed in 1870, at a time when Bahá'u'lláh was still imprisoned in the horrible confines of 'Akká. This was when its original owner observed to one of the learned scholars there that he would like a special verse created for the entrance marker. Such markers were used in much the same way as the engraved cornerstones that are legend in historical American buildings.

Today you can still read this verse engraved in marble over the entrance of the House at Bahjí. It is amazingly prophetic, when you consider the time in which it was written!

O Mansion, upon Thee be greetings and peace
the days will shed their lights upon you through the ages
in this Mansion
through strange and wonderful things
the pens of the world
are at a loss to describe.

It was while Bahá'u'lláh lived at Bahjí in the year 1890 that He was visited by the late Professor Edward G. Browne, of the University of Cambridge, who was distinguished for his Oriental knowledge. Professor Brown later noted how deeply impressed he had been at this meeting:

. . . In the corner where the divan met the wall sat a wondrous and venerable figure, crowned with a felt headdress of the kind called táj . . . , round the base of which was wound a small white turban. The face of him on whom I gazed I can never forget, though I cannot describe it. Those piercing eyes seemed to read one's very soul; power and authority sat on that ample brow; while the deep lines on the forehead and face implied an age which the jet-black hair and beard flowing down in indistinguishable luxuriance almost to the waist seemed to belie. No need to ask in whose presence I stood, as I bowed myself before one who is the object of a devotion and love which kings might envy and emperors sigh for in vain!

That same "piercing" gaze was also to be one of the strongest impressions visitors of 'Abdu'l-Bahá would take away with them in the future.

The House at Bahjí went through many travails after the Bahá'ís bought it, but today it is one of their Holy Shrines, to which the Bahá'í pilgrims go when they have the privilege of visiting Israel. The Touch of not only Bahá'u'lláh and 'Abdu'l-

Bahá is upon the mementoes there, but also the imprint of the loving care with which Bahá'u'lláh's great-grandson, Shoghi Effendi, restored its interior beauty and made come true many of the gardens and other aspirations that 'Abdu'l-Bahá had for Bahjí.

Bahá'u'lláh lived nine years in the city of 'Akká, two years in Mazra'ih (with visits to the Gardens) and thirteen years in the Mansion at Bahjí, including other visits to the Gardens.

His long imprisonment, His trials, and His tribulations eventually took their toll upon Him. He had a fever for only a day at the Mansion in Bahjí and later that same day seemed to be recovering.

But that night—it was actually after midnight of May 29, 1892—Bahà'u'llàh slipped away from this world's hold upon Him, from all the troubles, disappointments, challenges, and exertions of His earthly turmoil.

He was seventy-six years old when He ascended. For at least another thousand years the Bahá'ís believe there can be no One to bring a new Revelation.

A Prince of Heaven had died, but a New Day had been born.

The Center of

the Covenant — 'Abdu'l-Bahá

The Divine Covenant

AFTER FORTY YEARS of Divinely dedicated service, Bahá'u'lláh, the Manifestation on earth of God for this Day, had passed on to the Kingdom of God. Not, however, before He had created the foundation for God's Kingdom here on earth.

At the time of His passing, Bahá'u'lláh's Mission here had actually been fulfilled. His arrival in the Holy Land under the orders of the Turkish Sultan had been the consummation of the Prophecy of the Jewish, Christian, and Muḥammadan Scriptures, and His imprisonment had not prevented Bahá'u'lláh from also fulfilling the rest of His Divine Mission.

Bahá'u'lláh's Legacy to the world was more than the history of a great religious Leader. It was a Pattern for the ages to come of how mankind could live and progress.

Bahá'u'lláh left over one hundred great books of His own Writings, destined eventually to be translated into many languages. He left, too, innumerable Tablets and Prayers devised by Him, which were to be used for the guidance of all peoples.

He left an Heir, 'Abdu'l-Bahá, His Eldest Son, to guide the Bahá'ís in this, their latest extremity. 'Abdu'l-Bahá's appointment included the task of interpreting many of Bahá'u'ullah's Writings, of being the Exemplar of His Faith and of being the Center of His Covenant. It was an appointment and responsibility without parallel.

Through 'Abdu'l-Bahá Divine Authority and Guidance would still exist for the Bahá'ís, even though their Manifestation, Bahá'u'lláh, no longer lived. Revelation may have ceased, but what had been created assured the development of a religious society without racial, national, or other dividing characteristics. It meant that the qualities necessary to complete such a task had been found in 'Abdu'l-Bahá by Bahá'u'lláh, and that the believers had more than written Words to help them; they were assured of a continuing Leadership, Divine in Origin, and far beyond human comprehension.

Picture the wisdom and foresight that went into Bahá'u'lláh's appointment of 'Abdu'l-Bahá and His establishment of a new social order. In this way Bahá'u'lláh had provided for the uninterrupted continuance of the providential elements in religion and had supplied the manner and materials through which mankind would be able to achieve progress and peace, if it so desired.

During Bahá'u'lláh's lifetime, He had expounded teachings far different from those of His predecessors. In addition to both the spiritual and social teachings a prophet brings, Bahá'u'lláh had given mankind a complete blueprint of how it could achieve world peace and the Kingdom of God on earth, and how there could be peaceful co-relation between all men. If Bahá'u'lláh's Plan were followed, it would mean the establishment not only of individual peace, but also of the unification of all the divergent peoples and nations of the earth as well.

Bahá'u'lláh's teachings are expressed in such purity of thought that they remain unobscured by any blinding misconceptions. They were planned this way, and far in advance, to remain unimpaired by human distortion, and should any changes be needed these will be accomplished through divine means, not under human impulse or tyranny, the Bahá'ís believe.

That is why Bahá'u'lláh's Last Will and Testament included

a Covenant in which He made clear that all Bahá'ís who were faithful to God in this age must turn to 'Abdu'l-Bahá as best fitted to show them how to practice these teachings.

This use of the term "Covenant" is not new to religion. The Old Testament actually means the Old Covenant. The New Testament is the New Covenant. All through the Bible can be found the promise of a still newer Covenant to be made in the "Latter Day, the fullness of time. . . ."

Such a Covenant, therefore, is a *conditional* agreement between God and man. The Covenant of religion enshrines a promise by God, the fruition of which depends upon the fulfillment by man of certain conditions.

In the Bahá'í Writings is found: "O son of Being, Love Me that I may love thee. If thou lovest Me not, My love can in no wise reach thee." This love is God's promise, the condition being that Man must love Him before the love can function. There is always the condition, which is what makes it a Covenant, rather than an out-and-out promise or a laid-down set of laws.

The Articles of God's Covenant are the laws of the Manifestation and new ones are revealed at the time of His coming by each of God's Chosen Messengers.

The Covenant with Abraham gave the glad tidings that through His seed all the nations of the world would be blessed. The Covenant with Moses included the Ten Commandments. When the early Christians followed the Covenant given by Christ in the Sermon on the Mount they became united into a truly wonderful brotherhood.

The succession of the various Manifestations of God is the central law of the religious development of the world and is the supreme teaching of the Covenant. The law of spiritual history is that every prophet of God makes a Covenant with His followers that they should obey His Successor, the One Whom God has willed to come after Him.

Each Covenant also tells man to await the next Manifestation. The Covenant Bahá'u'lláh made with the Bahá'ís has to do with the establishment of the Kingdom of God on earth, the conditions of its establishment being the pure and selfless dedication and obedience of the believers. These are the conditions of the Covenant of God in this age.

In Baha'u'llah's Covenant with the Bahá'ís, the Baha'ís are told: "Because all men are created different, the opinions of men vary greatly. It is for this reason that there must exist some absolute standard by which men can be reconciled. . . . It is solely through the Covenant of Bahá'u'lláh that this standard will be upraised and maintained. . . ."

A law by itself is *not* a Covenant. It is when a law, to be fulfilled, is dependent upon obedience that it becomes a Covenant, and not until then.

In further explanation, 'Abdu'l-Bahá has written: "His Holiness Abraham, on Him be peace, made a covenant concerning His Holiness Moses and gave the glad tidings of His coming. His Holiness Moses made a covenant concerning the Promised One, i.e., His Holiness Christ, and announced the news of His Manifestation to the world. His Holiness Christ made a covenant concerning the Paraclet and gave the tidings of His coming. His Holiness, the Prophet Muḥammad, made a covenant concerning His Holiness the Báb and the Báb was the One promised by Muḥammad, for Muḥammad gave the tidings of His coming. The Báb made a covenant concerning the Blessed Beauty of Bahá'u'lláh and gave the glad-tidings of His coming. . . . Bahá'u'lláh made a covenant concerning a promised One who will become manifest after one thousand, or thousands, of years."

However, the Bahá'ís feel that former Covenants did not state as clearly the facts that Bahá'u'lláh's did, such as His Successor. Although the implication appears obvious that Peter was the primal point in Jesus' Covenant, Christ did not say explicitly, without leaving any doubt, that Peter was His Covenant's Center and the sole Interpreter of His teaching. Nor was Muḥammad able to leave His directions so firmly phrased as to prevent the splitting of the Faith of Islám into so many sects when He had passed on.

Bahá'u'lláh, however, *was* specific. Through the use of such phrases as "the object of this sacred verse is none other except the Most Mighty Branch" (one of His titles for 'Abdu'l-Bahá), expressed firmly in His Will and Testament, which was also Bahá'u'lláh's Covenant, the meaning was unmistakable.

The naming of Bahá'u'lláh's Successor was only one part of the Covenant He made with the Bahá'ís. A Covenant also has within it the power to help the Successor to fulfill what He is meant to do as the Manifestation's Heir. Through 'Abdu'l-Bahá's future destiny, planned by Bahá'u'lláh, He was ordained to help lay the foundation of the Bahá'í Administrative Order and to inspire the believers to carry eventually their teachings into every corner of this planet.

There is nothing in any other great religion to compare with Bahá'u'lláh's Covenant with His people. There is nothing in any previous Covenant that confers the undisputed authority that Bahá'u'lláh's Will conferred upon 'Abdu'l-Bahá, making certain that no one else was empowered to interpret the Bahá'í Faith or to manage its affairs.

No other religion has had such written confirmations of what its founder wanted done by his successor, and no other religion has anything approaching the detailed injunctions, laws, and warnings that came from the pens of both Bahá'u'lláh and 'Abdu'l-Bahá.

This clear appointment of 'Abdu'l-Bahá as the Center of the Covenant after Bahá'u'lláh's passing was to the Bahá'ís their strongest remaining channel and connection with holy and divine truth. Although they had lost Bahá'u'lláh, they still had the continuity of His purpose and Plan in 'Abdu'l-Bahá.

"We have made Thee a shelter for all mankind," Bahá'u'lláh attested, in writing, to His eldest Son, "a shield unto all who are in heaven and on earth, a stronghold for whoever hath believed in God, the incomparable, the All-Knowing. God grant that through Thee He may protect them, may enrich and sustain them, that He may inspire Thee with that which shall be a wellspring of wealth unto all created things, an ocean of bounty unto all men, and the dayspring of mercy unto all peoples."

'Abdu'l-Bahá had been deliberately called the "Mystery of God" by His Father, Bahá'u'lláh, and while it does not mean that 'Abdu'l-Bahá was by any means a prophet, it did indicate that He was a human being and in possession of certain divine attributes which gave Him both a knowledge and perfection that were different from those possessed by any other person.

One of the sacred and necessary duties facing 'Abdu'l-Bahá after the passing of Bahá'u'lláh was to make certain that the Bahá'í teachings would remain free from human interpretation and division, that schisms like those of other religious groups would not take place in the Bahá'í world.

His protection in all this was that the Revelation of Bahá'u'-lláh was complete in every possible detail before its Founder had died. 'Abdu'l-Bahá did not have to add anything to the laws, the regulations, the principles, the Institutions or the Guidance. These were divinely inspired and divinely revealed by Bahá'u'-lláh. 'Abdu'l-Bahá interpreted them, arranged for their adoption and use by the Bahá'ís at the time when the believers were at last ready to make adequate use of them, and made certain that, after His own death, the Will of God, expressed in Bahá'u'lláh's Covenant with the followers of the Faith, would continue to be followed by the obedient Bahá'ís of the future.

'Abdu'l-Bahá—The Master, the Exemplar

BAHA'U'LLAH, like every other Divine Founder of a Prophetic Dispensation, brought to the world a capacity in Himself for the complete reflection of the Will of God.

The outstanding teaching of Lao-tze was reverence, and today, many thousands of years later, the Chinese people are known as the most reverent of all races.

The identifying characteristic of the teachings of Brahma was sacrifice, and his followers still practice this to accomplish soul-purification.

Zoroaster stressed purity, and in the districts where this religion predominates, the Parsees give the lowest percentage of trouble, morally speaking, even less than any other Oriental group.

Buddha taught renunciation, a quality that his followers put foremost, which may be one reason for the Buddhists' being less opposed to other religions than any other major religious group beside the Bahá'ís, since the Buddhists renounce even a claim to an exclusive Revelation.

The Mission of Moses was directly concerned with righteousness, and his followers have obeyed his laws most consistently, and those very laws constitute the basis of practically all the laws existent in the world today.

Jesus emphasized the quality of love, and this particular principle is clearly and scientifically applied by most Christian peoples.

Muḥammad brought to his followers the law of submission, which they followed strictly, even though many Muḥammadans started out as members of lawless, barbaric tribes.

Finally Bahá'u'lláh brought His definitive principle of unity as the healing balm for all of man's spiritual ills and woes. He left a Mandate for the unification of all the schools of religion under the one banner of a single God, a gathering together of all God's worshipers under one roof, recognizing as Divine in its inception and origin each Prophetic Dispensation of the past, that all were ordained by the Almighty God for the expression of His Will.

The uniqueness, the universality, and the potential strength of the Bahá'í beliefs were stressed in all of Bahá'u'lláh's Messages, as the purpose and character of His Faith unfolded. Bahá'u'lláh even disclosed the significance behind His own sufferings and banishments, saying that they foreshadowed the glories and wonders in store for the Bahá'í Dispensation.

He recounted many moving and marvelous episodes of the various states in His Ministry and emphasized the transitory character of worldly pomp, fame, riches, and sovereignty. Often He appealed for the application of the highest principles in human and international relations and the abandonment of discreditable practices and conventions, pointing out how detrimental the latter were to the happiness, growth, prosperity, and unity of the entire human race.

This, then, was Bahá'u'lláh's Legacy to 'Abdu'l-Bahá, the theme on which His Son would elaborate, the goal 'Abdu'l-Bahá would have to give to the entire universe. All of Bahá'u'lláh's hopes, ideals, teachings, and plans would have to be recited, promoted, reinforced, and constantly re-emphasized by 'Abdu'l-Bahá.

In the early years of this century the Master wrote and lectured to audiences in Europe and North America, warning them of the deadly consequences of racial prejudice. Often He warned, a great destruction would come to mankind unless its peoples followed in God's way. As man well knows, in many areas His forebodings have already come to pass.

'Abdu'l-Bahá impressed upon the Bahá'ís that prestige in this world is of no importance, that those who are the highest may become the lowest and vice-versa. He told of the great Rabbi Caiaphas who became abased, whereas the humble Peter became greatly elevated spiritually. He reminded them that Mary the Magdalen, even though an adultress, was promoted to a lofty spiritual station. His moral was that since a Manifestation of God is empowered to perform whatever God willeth, the man or soul who outwardly is nothing can be made everything by God.

History proves that members of the Ottoman Turkish Government who had treated Bahá'u'lláh and His entourage so shamefully later became exiles themselves, whereas those who had been punished by that government for kindness to these special prisoners were later promoted to high government posts.

'Abdu'l-Bahá has told of the time in Europe when He met a member of the British Parliament.

> He asked me: "What is the proof of His Holiness, Bahá-'u'lláh? I want it in a concise and useful form." I said: "The concise and sufficient proof is that Bahá'u'lláh in such a prison as Acre, and when under chains, raised His banner. In Ṭihrán He was in prison and under chains. In Acre He was in prison. Under these circumstances He raised His banner." When I mentioned this proof he became very silent. I said: "There is nothing recorded comparable to this. What power is this, that from the beginning of the world until today such a thing has not happened?"

From the beginning of the world until today there has not been recorded any other such person as 'Abdu'l-Bahá. Infallible because Bahá'u'lláh, the Manifestation of God, had decreed that He be so, He was still human, although always divinely inspired and divinely motivated.

It had been obvious from the time He was a small child that somehow He was different from all other children. He had been born on the night when the Báb declared His Mission to Mullá Ḥusayn. While still very young, 'Abdu'l-Bahá had recognized the Glory of His Father's as yet unrevealed Station and had begged the privilege of laying down His life for Bahá'u'lláh's sake. He had devoted Himself to the service of Bahá'u'lláh and the Faith from that time. His swift knowledge and His great help in such practical matters as contacting government officials and acting as Deputy for His Father in many ways had increasingly earned Him a love and respect from Bahá'ís and non-Bahá'ís which was only second to that given to Bahá'u'lláh.

As a mere boy 'Abdu'l-Bahá had been privileged to meet Ṭáhirih, the poetess who was the Báb's only female Letter of the Living. As a youth He had the dreadful experience of beholding Bahá'u'lláh weighed down with chains in the horrible Black Hole of Síyáh-Chál, when permitted to visit His beloved Father there. Often He was the object of malice and ridicule from other children, and He consequently matured much earlier than most boys did, taking on many of the responsibilities for His distraught family due to His Father's preoccupation or periodic imprisonments.

He accompanied Bahá'u'lláh in the long banishment from their native land, and grew up as a prisoner in 'Akká, concentrating always on ways to help His Father and the other believers with them. He performed all the business chores, arranged interviews with the pilgrims and government officials and protected Bahá'u'lláh in many ways. When allowed more freedom to roam beyond the prison walls, He got to know the troubles and problems of the native inhabitants of the City, and after Bahá'u'lláh became a resident of Mazra'ih and Bahjí, it was 'Abdu'l-Bahá Who acted as messenger and go-between for His Father.

Like the Báb and Bahá'u'lláh (despite not being accorded the Station of a Prophet) 'Abdu'l-Bahá had innate knowledge of many phases of human relations which He had not been formally taught. Time and again He pleaded fluently to officials on behalf of Bahá'u'lláh and the Cause. It was Bahá'u'lláh Who requested that 'Abdu'l-Bahá work out all the negotiations for the purchase and acquisition of the Haifa lands which eventually became the spiritual and administrative headquarters of the fast-expanding Bahá'í administrative order.

When 'Abdu'l-Bahá became His Father's Successor, the Center of His Covenant, He imparted an extraordinary impetus to the Faith, gradually destroying any and every barrier that threatened to impede its progress. During His own lifetime He was able to implement Bahá'u'lláh's Tablets and Instruction into the foundation of a truly unique World Order, planned to one day signal the advent of the Golden Age of the Bahá'í Dispensation.

'Abdu'l-Bahá often worked tirelessly and endlessly, and it seemed there was no limit to the demands that could be made upon His strength and time. From His lips and pen streamed volumes of documents, letters, Tablets, prayers, interpretations, supplementations—all inspired by the Example, Writings, and Knowledge given Him by Bahá'u'lláh.

'Abdu'l-Bahá never permitted anyone to believe or act as though He Himself was a Manifestation of God. His responsibility lay in fulfilling Bahá'u'lláh's Will and Testament, in continuing Bahá'u'lláh's work, but He could not start anything not already willed by God and the Manifestation. The Bahá'í Pattern was already clearly there, in writing, a Testament that was uniquely Bahá'u'lláh's.

During His time in 'Akká, while Bahá'u'lláh lived in Bahjí, 'Abdu'l-Bahá was a continual source of amazement to His family and visiting Bahá'ís. They were astonished at His never-ending goodness to all and His constant flow of concern for everyone's welfare. He would forget to eat or sleep in His anxiety over those living in 'Akká, and would have to make certain first that *they* had food and a place to rest their weary heads. One Persian friend described this aspect of the Master: "There is not an alley in 'Akká I do not know, nor a prison cell, for I have followed the footsteps of my Lord."

Each Friday He would welome the sick, the lame, the halt, the blind, and the lepers, giving them alms and loving kindness because He felt that words were not enough for the poor when they needed greater proof of individual concern.

Bahá'u'lláh's death didn't bring an end to the hate and resentment felt by the enemies of the Cause. They finally succeeded in renewing the suspicions of the Turkish officials against the Bahá'ís and one of 'Abdu'l-Bahá's friends stealthily came to warn Him to leave. The Sultan was sending an investigating committee from Constantinople to try Him for treason, and far in advance they had decided to pronounce Him guilty. The Spanish consul offered to spirit the Master away on an Italian ship, but He refused.

"The Báb did not run away; Bahá'u'lláh did not run away, and now neither will I run away. I will not deliver myself. . . ."

Although the spectre of banishment or worse prevailed,

'Abdu'l-Bahá remained outwardly calm and confident. He surprised both His friends and His enemies by ordering His
gardener to pluck the flowers and fruits of the garden to present
to anyone who might call upon Him.

His confidence in God's Will was rewarded. At the moment
when it seemed as though calamity was surely upon Him and
the believers, the news came that the ship which had delivered
the investigating committee and planned to take 'Abdu'l-Bahá
back with them, this same ship had departed with this committee,
but without any reason announced for the departure. It was later
learned that the Young Turks had tried to kill the Sultan in
Constantinople and such an uprising was of more immediate
importance to the Ottoman Government than anything a group
of so-called religious rebels might do.

Finally, to the joy of the oppressed, the Revolution of the
Young Turks was overwhelmingly successful. All the political
and religious prisoners of the Turkish Empire were released,
which, of course, included the Bahá'ís.

After what must have seemed like a lifetime of confinement,
'Abdu'l-Bahá was free. He could live where He wished, work as
He desired, He could even travel when so inclined. It was the year
1908 and after forty years the Son of Bahá'u'lláh was to have
His first true taste of freedom.

He wanted very much to fulfill two tasks that were actually
Self-ordained. The first was to entomb the remains of the Báb
on the side of Mount Carmel in Haifa where 'Abdu'l-Bahá and
the Bahá'í Holy Family now lived. The second was to visit
personally the areas of the Western World where the teachings
were to rise and be known by as many people as possible. It
would be a couple of years before either of these plans could be
realized.

Meanwhile, 'Abdu'l-Bahá wrote and inspired vast Bahá'í
teaching strides throughout the universe. As Bahá'í teachers
developed, He had them pioneer to other lands, some far away,
to bring the Message of Bahá'u'lláh to those deprived areas of

the world which needed it badly. Many of these Bahá'í traveling teachers came from the United States, where the Faith had its first believer in 1894. By 1898 American pilgrims began to visit 'Akká and made themselves known to 'Abdu'l-Bahá as the nucleus of His future expansion of the teachings in North America, which included Canada.

One young woman in this initial group was named May Bolles. In 1902 she married a prominent Canadian architect, Sutherland Maxwell, and they eventually became great friends of 'Abdu'l-Bahá and wonderful teachers for the Faith. From this union came a daughter, Mary Maxwell, who many years later was to become the wife of 'Abdu'l-Bahá's grandson, Shoghi Effendi.

Until then, it was 'Abdu'l-Bahá's task to help shape the Administrative Order of the Faith, guide its beginnings in many countries, watch the creation and progress of the local and national Bahá'í assemblies upon which the future international administration would depend. Through 'Abdu'l-Bahá's efforts, the formative and evolutionary spirit of the Bahá'í Dispensation was able to carry forward Bahá'u'lláh's Plan without interruption, helping to preserve its fundamental aim and character for all time.

There were now many new Bahá'í centers throughout the Western World. The believers there were pleading for 'Abdu'l-Bahá to visit them. His health had at last broken under the strain of imprisonment and suffering and He was nearing His seventieth birthday. He knew little of Western languages and He had never before talked in public to large groups. Nevertheless He accepted the challenge of what lay ahead and in 1910 began to prepare for this long journey.

He started out from Egypt but became ill and had to return there. The following autumn He was able to visit London and Paris, then sailed in the spring of 1912 for the United States and Canada. He was to remain in North America for some eight months and visit more Bahá'í areas in Europe before seeing Haifa again.

Picture, if one can, this wonderful Soul, frail but determined, this Source of all good for the believers of the infant Bahá'í Faith, so insistent that nothing could stop His personal encouragement of the wonderful new believers in the Western World.

'Abdu'l-Bahá in North America

AMERICA at the turn of the century was not the way it is now. She was only beginning to become a burgeoning world power. Her people were still confused about their country's nickname, "the melting pot of the world." Too many divergent races, religions, ideas, and peoples were beginning to cram her borders and while there were many alert souls who recognized the Bahá'í Message as one of Unity, there were still not enough Bahá'ís in the United States at the time to make it a popular credo.

Mrs. Phoebe Hearst, grandmother of the present Hearst clan, was among those who helped to bring the Bahá'í teachings to America. Her picture is on the wall of Bahá'u'lláh's Mansion at Bahjí. Among those she brought into the Faith was her butler, Mr. Turner. When they visited 'Abdu'l-Bahá with one of the first groups of American pilgrims, Mr. Turner insisted on waiting outside, as was expected of a servant in those days. 'Abdu'l-Bahá insisted too, and went out to bring him inside, then talked only to him. This offended no one, as they understood the Master's idea of demonstrating humility and equality of mankind.

When tea was served, 'Abdu'l-Bahá motioned to His attendants to serve Mr. Turner first. Later He wrote a Tablet about the beauty of Mr. Turner's face and spirit, which included the observation, "I shall come to you in a dream and I shall convey to you a Message." Mr. Turner became the first Negro Bahá'í.

Because Americans were so primarily concerned with economic values and had been accustomed to thinking in terms of pride and prejudice, 'Abdu'l-Bahá made a special point of helping the American Bahá'ís to feel differently. He advised:

> ... No Bahá'í must open his lips in blaming another one; he must regard backbiting as the greatest sin of humanity, for it is clearly revealed in all the Tablets of Bahá'u'lláh that back-biting and fault-finding are the fiendish instruments and suggestions of Satan and the destroyers of the foundation of man.
>
> A believer will not blame any soul among the strangers, how much less against the friends. Fault-finding and backbiting are the characteristics of the weak minds and not the friends. Self-exaltation is the attribute of the stranger and not of the Beloved.
>
> It is our hope that the believers and the maid-servants of the Merciful in America may become the cause of the union of the East and the West, and unfurl the Standard of the Oneness of the Realm of Humanity. ...

The American believers were so delighted to have their beloved Master visit them that they pleaded to pay His expenses, which He would not permit. He returned their offering with His love and blessing, and suggested that it be donated to some worthy charity, instead. All during His visit to the United States and Canada, He became known for His many generous gifts to the poor in the Bowery and elsewhere.

It was April 11, 1912, when 'Abdu'l-Bahá arrived in New York City on the SS *Cedric* from Egypt. A newspaper write-up of His appearance on the *Cedric* depicts Him to have been of medium height, looking even taller than He really was, as He paced the deck talking with reporters. He appeared alert and active, His head thrown back and splendidly poised upon His broad, square shoulders, while a profusion of iron-gray hair burst out at the sides of His turban and hung long upon His neck.

He had a large, massive head, full-domed and remarkably wide across the forehead and temples. His eyes were very wide apart, their orbs large and deep, looking out from under massive, overhanging brows. He had a strong Roman nose, a decisive yet kindly mouth and chin, and a creamy white complexion. His beard was the same color as his hair, worn full over the face and carefully trimmed to almost the same length.

'Abdu'l-Bahá explained that His mission was to travel as far as possible to every part of America, through cities and towns, telling everyone about the Faith. He was quoted as saying, "This is the outpouring of the wonderful and new springtime and the falling of the showers of the Bounty of the Most Great Lord!"

His talks in Europe had already presaged what He wanted the Americans to know. "Let those who meet you know without your saying that you are a Bahá'í." he exhorted. "You must manifest the most sincere love for all. Your hearts must burn with love for all. Let the people see that you are filled with universal love. If you meet a Persian, talk with him without ceremony, ask where he lives and try to help him. Likewise speak to all strangers who seem lonely, and try to give them your willing service.

"Be loving to them . . ." He had continued. "If they are poor, help them with money; if they are sad, comfort them; if they are distraught, quiet them; till all the world shall see that you have in truth the universal love. It is all very well for you to say that you agree with all this, that is good—but you must put it into practice."

During His visit to Washington, D. C., when women were trying to get the voting franchise in the United States, one female identified herself with the so-called stonger sex by cutting her hair very short and adopting men's clothing to wear.

When she heard that 'Abdu'l-Bahá was in the city, she rushed to see Him and pumped His hand forcefully, saying excitedly:

"I have always wanted to meet a Prophet of God."

"I am *not* a Prophet," corrected the Master politely. "I am only the Servant of God."

The woman paid Him no heed. "I have always wanted to meet a Prophet of God," she repeated.

'Abdu'l-Bahá was always known for His sense of humor.

Now His eyes sparkled, as He said: "I am *not* a Prophet. I am only a man—like you. . . ."

He attended all kinds of American Government functions during His tour in the States, and was entertained as the high-ranking visiting Dignitary He was. He met all sorts of highly placed individuals, and, at one elegant reception for Admiral Peary, 'Abdu'l-Bahá remained very still during His introduction to the explorer, who was very proud of his own feat.

Softly 'Abdu'l-Bahá observed:

"Admiral Peary? You have just been to the North Pole? And what did you find there? Nothing . . . I presume?"

One Bahá'í lady remembers that, when she was a child, she and her mother were the house guests of another Bahá'í in Chicago, during 'Abdu'l-Bahá's visit to that great city.

"Oh, how I would love to have a tea for you, 'Abdu'l-Bahá," this child's mother said when she met Him.

"That will be very pleasing to Me," He answered kindly, "if you will have guests, also, from the colored race."

Feeling honored and privileged by this granting of her request, the lady rushed back to her hostess with 'Abdu'l-Bahá's instructions. She was very surprised on the day of the event to learn that the guest list included only very social, wealthy, white friends of her hostess, but none from the Negro race, as the Master had requested.

A short time before the party was to start, a note came from 'Abdu'l-Bahá stating only that He would be unable to attend. The hostess looked at her friend in blank dismay.

"I wouldn't be surprised if 'Abdu'l-Bahá instinctively realizes you have disobeyed Him," her friend remarked, with complete faith in His innate knowledge. "I am sure that if you were to include some guests from the colored race, He would change His mind. . . ."

The lady of the house went into the kitchen and begged her Negro cook to have some of the cook's friends at the house by two that day. Sure enough, without having received this information from anyone, when they were all assembled, including the Negro guests, 'Abdu'l-Bahá arrived and mingled with everyone.

When He visited New York, He first stayed at a hotel where He believed there were no racial restrictions on visitors. Instead, the neighborhood people became greatly disturbed and told the hotel owner who, being afraid his future business might be impaired, went to 'Abdu'l-Bahá with the complaints. Without a word the Master packed and stayed with other friends until He had found a different hotel that showed no prejudice. He was known never to give an inch on any matter concerning Bahá'í principles.

Mr. Louis Gregory was a wonderful American Bahá'í who became the first Negro to be honored in the Faith for his many services and attributes. This talented and well-educated gentleman was highly attuned spiritually, and was especially regarded by 'Abdu'l-Bahá. The Master knew the resentments that various dinner guests might feel towards someone of Mr. Gregory's color. During a very important dinner party in Washington, D.C., at which a number of non-Bahá'í high-ranking government officials were present, 'Abdu'l-Bahá requested that the seat at His right be left vacant. Everyone wondered in low whispers for whom the seat was being reserved.

"Mr. Louis Gregory," came the announcement, as 'Abdu'l-Bahá rose to greet His new guest with warmth and dignity. The guests present realized that they had been given a very subtle but clear lesson by the Bahá'í Leader, as He sat His friend in the vacant chair. No prejudice of any kind could be permitted to exist in Bahá'í circles.

The afternoon of His arrival in San Francisco, 'Abdu'l-Bahá crossed the Bay to Oakland where, after finishing a talk for the adults, He took the children into His arms, embracing and blessing them. They felt His love and pattered after Him into the next room. One dear little girl wanted to know whether she would be allowed to "pet the God-man."

He spoke to a group at the Japanese Young Men's Christian Association in Oakland, and when He passed down the aisle to leave, mothers held out their babies for His blessing. They all smiled radiantly when He said in carefully prepared English, "Good baby, Japanese baby."

When He visited Stanford University in Palo Alto for a day, He was enthusiastically greeted by the fifteen hundred students waiting for him there. One group from another school walked five miles each way, after making the thirty-mile train trip to hear Him. As they took the very late train to return to their homes, they all agreed: "We are well repaid—more than repaid—and all very happy."

In Berkeley, California, besides giving a public address, he made a private visit to the humble home of a Negro Bahá'í who was confined there with a broken leg. Wherever He went, His majestic figure stood out, and people got to know Him from the newspaper photographs and announcements. He greeted everyone, friend or stranger, in well-rehearsed English, with "Good morning? How are you? Are you well? Are you happy? Very happy?"

When they would answer or nod their heads "yes," to show they were happy, He would again reply in good English, "Very well? Very happy? All right?" Those fortunate enough to hear would say how He laughed at their own joy.

During His public talks or interviews, however, He had an interpreter and would talk in an easy unrehearsed flow of words in His native language, Persian.

One woman, who was a young child when He came to America, said that she learned a very great lesson from 'Abdu'l-Bahá. Her father visited Him in Haifa before dying unexpectedly, and her mother had corresponded with the Master. The mother and child were therefore very pleased to be granted an audience when He arrived in their city.

At that time it was the annual custom to make May Day baskets. Little Rene made one for 'Abdu'l-Bahá, but had forgotten to take out the needle when she finished sewing. Her mother bought some lovely flowers and filled up the basket, but as they approached Him, 'Abdu'l-Bahá swept the little girl into His arms. He didn't realize the basket was there and that it became nearly crushed. He just repeated over and over again, with her in His arms, "Howard's child, Howard's child."

The little girl felt like crying when she saw that there were many larger and finer baskets of flowers standing all over the room, but was happy again when 'Abdu'l-Bahá accepted her crushed offering as though it were the only one He had received.

Outside the hotel apartment once more, the little girl's mother suggested that they wait for a while, in the hope of seeing Him walk by later. Another little girl with her mother went into the suite, and when they came out the second child was clutching the very basket the first one had given to 'Abdu'l-Baha!

She thought her heart would break and ignored the thought that perhaps 'Abdu'l-Bahá had nothing else around to please a little girl. Years later she understood that perhaps 'Abdu'l-Bahá innately knew that she and her mother were waiting outside and had tried also to give her the gift of generosity.

'Abdu'l-Bahá's visit to the Green Acre Bahá'í School located at Eliot, Maine, is remembered and commemorated in part by their keeping intact the room in which He stayed during His never-to-be-forgotten week there. Visiting Bahá'ís and even non-Bahá'ís can enter it any hour of the day or night to pray or meditate and to feel the wonder of being in the spot where He had been so many years before.

They also walk through the path of pines where His feet had trod, and seek out the noble elevation called Mount Salvat that 'Abdu'l-Bahá had prophesied would some day be the site of the first American Bahá'í University. They love to sit under the trees as He had, remembering stories of how He had talked with the new believers at that time who would never forget how very privileged they had been to hear Him.

Green Acre originally developed from the spiritual quest of a high-minded lady named Sarah Farmer. The main building is named Sarah Farmer Hall, but it was called something else when a group of local businessmen first planned it as a hotel. Somehow it never seemed to prosper under their management.

Miss Farmer was a spiritually inclined person who had a feeling about the place: that she could use it to teach comparative religions to other inquiring minds. In 1893 she heard about the Bahá'í Faith while attending the Congress of World Religions in Chicago, and, as her interest in the teachings deepened, the concentration of the school curriculum turned to the subject of "the ascertainment of Truth and its helpful application in life."

It was after she visited 'Abdu'l-Bahá in 1899, as a pilgrim, that she become completely dedicated to the Bahá'í principles and when she returned to Green Acre the school was turned over entirely to the Faith. Since then the emphasis there has been on the teachings, and the "Persian Pine" on the grounds of Green Acre is where Miss Farmer used to hold regular lectures on Bahá'u'lláh's Revelation.

When 'Abdu'l-Bahá visited there in August 1912, Green Acre's founder was ill in a nursing home, where He went to see her. He impressed upon the students of the school, as well as upon future Bahá'ís, that Sarah Farmer was a true teacher of the Faith and a very wonderful person.

Later he wrote in a letter that He desired the Bahá'ís to make of Green Acre "an assemblage for the Word of God and a gathering place for the spiritual ones of the heavenly world."

Sarah Farmer died in 1916. The Green Acre school is now directed by a special Bahá'í Council under the supervision of the National Assembly of Bahá'ís of the United States, and its summer courses are attended by Bahá'ís and interested seekers from all parts of North America.

Many believers have built cottages on the grounds to be used by pupils attending Green Acre sessions, and the prices for food and lodging are the lowest one could hope for. There is a self-help work program by the students of all ages in order to keep the Green Acre physical properties maintained in good condition. The school has a capacity attendance of two hundred persons and nonmembers are invited to participate, to observe how happily Bahá'ís can live together with people from all countries, races, and backgrounds.

It is amazing to realize the varied and immense schedule the Master undertook despite His broken health and advanced years. There are many stories handed down in books and stories told of the efforts believers and nonbelievers made to meet Him during His months in North America.

One young man rode lying on the rods between the wheels of a train to Maine from Minneapolis, because he could not afford a train ticket. A mother of a young child was shown 'Abdu'l-Bahá's picture in a window of a store and realized it was He she had dreamed of and immediately rushed to travel to where He was.

There were a number of remarkable meetings 'Abdu'l-Bahá had with churchmen of many denominations. He impressed them all with His loving kindness, humility, and power of attraction. The people and congregations of all Faiths acclaimed Him when He spoke in their own houses of worship.

No one can adequately describe 'Abdu'l-Bahá's visits or their results, especially those who know these only from hearsay. Shoghi Effendi gave an account, however, in one of the Bahá'í books:

Who knows what thoughts flooded the heart of 'Abdu'l-Bahá as He found Himself the central Figure of such memorable scenes as these? . . . As He listened . . . to the hymns of thanksgiving and praise that would herald His approach to the numerous and brilliant assemblages of His enthusiastic followers and friends organized in so many cities of the

American continent? Who knows what memories stirred within Him as He stood before the thundering waters of Niagara, breathing the free air of a distant land, or gazed, in the course of a brief and much-needed rest, upon the green woods and countryside in Glenwood Springs, or moved with a retinue of Oriental believers along the paths of the Trocadero Gardens in Paris, or walked alone in the evening beside the majestic Hudson on Riverside Drive in New York . . . ?

. . . Memories of the sorrows, the poverty, the overhanging doom of His earlier years; memories of His mother who sold her gold buttons to provide Him, His brother, and His sister with sustenance, and who was forced, in her darkest hours, to place a handful of dry flour in the palm of His hand to appease His hunger. . . .

Above all, His thoughts must have entered on Bahá'u'lláh, Whom He loved so passionately and Whose trials He had witnessed and had shared from His boyhood . . . pictures from the tragic past such as these must have many a time overpowered Him with feelings of mingled gratitude and sorrow, as He witnessed the many marks of respect, of esteem and honor now shown Him and the Faith which He represented. . . .

His North American tour carried Him from coast to coast and in the course of it He visited Washington, Chicago, Cleveland, Pittsburgh, Montclair, Boston, Worcester, Brooklyn, Fanwood, Milford, Philadelphia, West Englewood, Jersey City, Cambridge Medford, Morristown, Dublin, Green Acre, Montreal, Malden, Buffalo, Kenosha, Minneapolis, St. Paul, Omaha, Lincoln, Denver, Glenwood Springs, Salt Lake City, San Francisco, Oakland, Palo Alto, Berkeley, Pasadena, Los Angeles, Sacramento, Cincinnati, and Baltimore.

In New York City alone He spent seventy-nine days. He made public addresses or formal visits in fifty-five different places, and His rooms were filled with visitors wherever He went, from early morning to late at night.

During the eight months, He addressed leading universities, attended conferences of all kinds, spoke before scientific organizations, socialistic bodies, welfare organizations. Every kind of religious place, women's clubs, colleges, metaphysical groups—

all willingly opened their doors to His Message. He was the guest of honor in leading mansions throughout America and at the lovely Maxwell Home in Montreal, Canada, which today is maintained as a Shrine in tribute to His visit. He spoke with all kinds of men and women, visited the homes of the poor as well as of the rich, and gave all of His appearances and talks without price, since He preferred to accept reward from none except God.

The American Bahá'ís felt singularly honored when He consented to lay the foundation stone of their great House of Worship (also called the Bahá'í Temple) on the shores of Lake Michigan at Wilmette, Illinois, near Chicago. It was the first edifice of a world religion that had been planned to be a sanctuary for people of all races, color, and Faiths, in the Western Hemisphere.

The stone used for the special ceremony was a fragment of limestone that had been painstakingly brought to the Temple site by Mrs. Nettie Tobin of Chicago, one of the first American believers. This stone is still displayed in a special room of the Foundation Hall of the Temple, where the Bahá'ís singly or a few at a time may go in for prayer and meditation.

Curiously, 'Abdu'l-Bahá's visit to New York was to bring a singular Bahá'í honor to another American community. One evening He was in the Tenth Street studio of the Manhattan believer Miss Juliet Thompson. She was painting His portrait. With them was one of His tour companions from abroad, another American, Mrs. Lua Getsinger. She had devoted her life to serving the Master. Suddenly He spoke:

"I am 'Abdu'l-Bahá and only 'Abdu'l-Bahá," He said in part, "and I am to be known as the Center of the Covenant. Go downstairs," pointing to Mrs. Getsinger, "and proclaim to the people of New York that I am the Center of the Covenant and that this is the City of the Covenant. . . ."

Ever since that time, the Bahá'ís of New York City have felt their special responsibility as members of the Bahá'í community which 'Abdu'l-Bahá named "The City of the Covenant," and visitors—Bahá'í or not—are made welcome at their public meetings each Friday night and Sunday afternoon.

'Abdu'l-Bahá's words of farewell in December 1912 to the believers, before He sailed from New York on the same boat that had brought Him there, were once more on the theme of unity and love for all:

"Beware lest ye offend any heart!" He cautioned the weeping believers, so grieved at the knowledge that He would soon be gone from their sight. "Beware lest ye speak against any one in his absence! You must consider all the servants of God as your own kith and kin. Let your whole effort be directed towards rejoicing every offended one, towards feeding every one who is hungry, clothing every one who is without clothing, glorifying every one who is humbled.

"Be a helper to every helpless one and be kind unto all. This is to gain the good will of God. This is that which is conducive to eternal felicity for you. This is conducive to the illumination of the world of humanity. As I seek from God eternal glory in your behalf, I therefore am giving you this exhortation. . . ."

Today, when the Bahá'ís of both the United States and Canada, who live in the special areas that were honored by visits from 'Abdu'l-Bahá at that time, want to do something very special for visitors, they have special "tours" and tell once more the glory that was their community's when the Master came to visit.

The Story of the End

A YEAR after 'Abdu'l-Bahá had returned to the Bahá'í international headquarters in Haifa, World War I began. He did all He could to help the inhabitants of the country which was still known as Palestine. Its citizens had many privations and problems but had ignored 'Abdu'l-Bahá's many hints concerning this coming holocaust. The Bahá'ís there, however, had heeded Him and had grown and stored what food they could, at His suggestion, so they could share it during the war with those in Palestine who were in need.

There were many hints of peril to both 'Abdu'l-Bahá and the Faith during those World War I years. The enemies of this fast-spreading religion were still trying to spread their hate around. Needless to say, such calamities were averted. When the British regime was established in Palestine, great friendship was shown to the Faith.

The British Government also knighted 'Abdu'l-Bahá in 1920 for His many services to the Palestinians during the war. Although He thanked them for the honor, He never used the title, nor did He permit it to be used for Him.

Until Friday, November 25, 1921, the Master followed the same loving, hard-working and charitable habits He always maintained in Haifa. On that day He attended the usual meeting of the Bahá'í friends in His audience chamber at His own house. The next morning He had developed a chill and asked for the fur coat belonging to Bahá'u'lláh, which He always wore when feeling cold or ailing. He then withdrew to His room and lay down, asking to be covered up because He had not slept well the previous night and was cold.

Shoghi Effendi, in collaboration with a devoted English Bahá'í, Lady Blomfeld, later gave many of the sad details in writing to Bahá'ís everywhere.

> That day He was rather feverish. In the evening His temperature rose still higher, but during the night the fever left Him. After midnight He asked for some tea. On Sunday morning, November 27, He said: "I am quite well and will get up as usual and have tea with you in the tea room," but after dressing He was persuaded to remain on the sofa in His room.
>
> At four in the afternoon He said: "Ask my sister and all the family to come and have tea with me." The same evening He asked after the health of every member of the household, of the pilgrims and of the friends in Haifa. "Very good, very good," He said, when told that none were ill. This was His very last utterance concerning His friends.

At eight in the evening He retired to bed after taking a little nourishment, saying, "I am quite well." He told all the family to go to bed and rest. Two of His daughters, however, stayed with Him. That night the Master had gone to sleep very calmly, quite free from fever.

He awoke about 1:15 A.M., got up and walked across to a table where He drank some water. He took off an outer garment, saying, "I am too warm." He want back to bed and when one of His daughters later on approached she found Him lying peacefully there. As He looked into her face He asked her to lift up the net curtains, saying, "I have difficulty in breathing; give me more air."

Some rose water was brought, of which He drank, sitting up in bed to do so, without any help. He again lay down, and as some food was offered Him He remarked in a clear and distinct voice, "You wish me to take some food and I am going?"

He gave them a beautiful look. His face was so calm, His expression so serene, they thought Him asleep.

His "sleep," however, was one from which He would never awaken.

"He had gone from the gaze of His loved ones!" the account ended.

Today, when Bahá'í pilgrims and visitors go to Haifa, one of the highlights of their visit is being allowed to visit the Master's House, which is where Ruhiyyih Khanum, the widow of the late Guardian, lives when she is in residence in Haifa.

They remove their shoes, and walk softly into 'Abdu'l-Bahá's bedroom where He died. They go in one or two at a time and they pray. The peace and beauty of the atmosphere makes them feel just a little more blessed, just a little more special for the rest of their lives, knowing they have been permitted to see His things and to feel that His Presence is still there.

'Abdu'l-Bahá has never gone from the hearts of His loved ones, only from their gaze. As long as the Bahá'í Faith lives, and it grows stronger every hour, so will the Master continue to live!

The Guardianship
of the Faith

The Last Rites for 'Abdu'l-Bahá

WHEN 'ABDU'L-BAHA died, He held a Supreme Station not only in the Bahá'í world, but in the world outside of it as well. On September 23, 1918, Lord Allenby, who was in charge of the British occupation of Palestine, followed a special order from the King of England to call and inquire about 'Abdu'l-Bahá's health. It was this same king who had once knighted the Master, bestowing upon Him his country's highest honor and the title of "Sir." 'Abdu'l-Bahá accepted the honor and title purely as a matter of diplomatic and natural courtesy.

The Master was considered by all who came in contact with Him as the true Example of virtue, purity, and the perfections. He was famous in both the East and the West for His dignity, kindness, patience, mercy, and wisdom, and He so demonstrated charity and generosity that He was described as "the hope of the hopeless, the help of the helpless."

His passing was recognized as a major catastrophe to Bahá'ís and non-Bahá'ís everywhere, and His absence was to leave an emptiness in the Bahá'í world comparable to nothing else since Bahá'u'lláh had departed.

Believers feel that there is much evidence that 'Abdu'l-Bahá must have known when He would die. He had openly hinted at His going, and daily would remind those around Him how very tired He felt.

He had seldom suffered from serious physical problems. He had contracted an occasional cold, or some other type of respiratory infection, but such ailments never really kept Him from His appointed duties and from fulfilling the work He felt must be done for the Faith.

Not until three days before His passing did He allow Himself to slow down even a little from His usual heavy schedule, and to rest on his bed more than usual.

He left behind His sister, known as "The Greatest Holy Leaf," His wife, four daughters, and numerous grandchildren. Shoghi Effendi had been particularly close to His grandfather, acting as His secretary. He had not known that, when 'Adul'h-Bahà was in 'Akká, technically imprisoned within the city walls, He had already written His Last Will and Testament in a series of three separate documents, and that Shoghi Effendi, then only a young schoolboy, was named therein as His Successor. Many years later the Guardian's wife explained to the believers that "it was also practically during the babyhood of . . . [Shoghi Effendi] that the Master revealed [a] highly significant Tablet about a child having been born who would do great things in the future. When asked by His secretary . . . whether by this was meant a living child or if it was a symbolical expression, the Master explained a real child was meant and that it would raise the Cause of God to great heights."

At nine o'clock on the morning of Tuesday, November 29, 1921, Allenby Road, the wide street near 'Abdu'l-Bahá's home was congested with the crowds standing quietly to pay homage to Him. The casket was of plain white wood covered with a precious Persian shawl. The procession moved slowly. In front, a company of police and their officers, then the Muḥammadan and the Christian Boy Scouts with band and flags, then the Personal Guards of the Consuls of all the Governments, with the leaders of the various Muḥammadan, Christian, and Jewish sects in front of the casket, chanting heart-touching hymns. Behind the casket marched the Governor-General of the Holy Land and the members of his staff.

The cortege took an hour and a half to move up Mount Carmel to arrive finally at the tomb of the Báb. The casket was placed on a dais, near the high and majestic tomb commanding the most beautiful view on Mount Carmel. The dignitaries, religious leaders, and Bahá'ís made a ring by standing around the casket, and, together with those who made up the balance of the procession, created a picture that Haifa had never before witnessed.

Eulogies were given by the top representatives of the various religious groups, all united by the Spirit of Love and Unity that 'Abdu'l-Bahá had pleaded for throughout His Life. One of the distinguished learned Muhammadans, Professor 'Abdu'lláh Effendi Mukhlis, expressed the feelings of many there in these tender poetic terms:

> Have you seen the sun set, the disappearance of the moon and the falling of the stars? Have you heard of the crumbling of the thrones, the leveling of the mountains? ... Yea, the Sun of Knowledge has set; the Moon of Virtues has disappeared; the Throne of Glory has crumbled and the Mountains of Kindness are leveled by the departure of this benevolent one from the mortal world to the immortal realm. ... Alas! Who will after him feed the hungry, clothe the naked, rescue the distressed, guide those astray, help the widows, and assist the orphans. ... This calamity has made all previous calamities to be forgotten. ... This calamity will never be forgotten. ...

After the funeral the Holy Family awaited the arrival of Shoghi Effendi, since nothing further could be undertaken until then regarding the reading of the Will and Testament.

What many Bahá'ís did not know was that in August 1918 the Master and His whole family had narrowly escaped crucifixion on Mount Carmel, a tragedy which had only been frustrated by the unexpectedly swift advance of Allenby's troops, forcing the Turkish authorities out of Haifa before they had time to carry out their terrible threat or take 'Abdu'l-Bahá and the members of His family into the hills as hostages.

The Bahá'ís did know, however, that 'Abdu'l-Bahá had instructed them:

> I say unto you that anyone who will rise up in the Cause of God at this time shall be filled with the Spirit of God and that He will send His Hosts from heaven to help you and that nothing shall be impossible to you if you have faith. And now I give you a commandment which shall be for a Covenant between you and me—that ye have faith, that your faith be steadfast as a rock that no storms can move, that nothing can disturb, and that it endure through all things even to the end; even should ye hear that your Lord has been crucified, be not shaken in your faith; for I am with you always, whether living or dead, I am with you to the end. As ye have faith so shall your powers and blessings be. This is the standard—this is the standard—this is the standard.

And this *was* the standard that helped all true believers during the dark days that followed. Particularly it must have helped Shoghi Effendi to bear the shock and surprise when he learned that his Grandfather's Last Will and Testament had indeed put him into a position that he had never sought or even imagined for himself, the Station of Guardian of the Cause throughout the world, for with this responsibility came also the task of molding the Administrative Order of the Faith, an administration that was fast becoming so necessary to the Faith's very life and future.

The Last Will and Testament of 'Abdu'l-Bahá

PART OF Shoghi Effendi's duty lay in emphasizing again and again in his future writings that while the Bahá'ís were to revere and respect 'Abdu'l-Bahá as a Singular Individual, they must follow His and Bahá'u'lláh's wishes by never confusing the Master with the Manifestation of God. Such a magnetic personality as 'Abdu'l-Bahá had fulfilled a unique function ordained through the Covenant of Bahà'u'llàh, so that, together with Bahá'u'lláh and the Báb, He had helped to formulate the framework of the Bahá'í Teachings.

Shoghi Effendi had to make it clear over and over to the believers and to those not of the Faith that together the Báb, Bahá-'u'lláh, and 'Abdu'l-Bahá stand unique in the world's spiritual history. 'Abdu'l-Bahá was primarily the Interpreter of the Báb's and Bahá'u'lláh's Teachings, and the Creator of the Document, His Last Will and Testament, which proclaimed Shoghi Effendi, His Grandson and Bahá'u'lláh's Great-Grandson, the Guardian of the Bahá'í Faith.

This Document detailed for the Bahá'ís all over the world, and for those who would become Bahá'ís later, the administrative pattern that Shoghi Effendi was empowered to develop. It consisted primarily of local and national Spiritual Assemblies and the Supreme Body, a Universal House of Justice. Such an administrative pattern had been planned by 'Abdu'l-Bahá as the indissoluble link for the true believers. It was meant to insure the continuity of the component parts of the Bahá'í Dispensation and would eventually be considered as the Charter of the new World Order which Bahá'ís had prepared for so long.

The believers have been taught to think of Bahá'u'lláh as providing the Principles and Purpose of their Faith, since these come from God. 'Abdu'l-Bahá has provided them with the Pattern, which is His Will and Testament, to ascertain that the eventual Administrative Order could provide the manner in which Bahá'u'lláh's Principles would be used in relation to human living. Last, the appointed Guardian, Shoghi Effendi, would supply the details of the Pattern for carrying out the Principles for Bahá'í action.

The mere reading, even today, of 'Abdu'l-Bahá's Last Will and Testament is a demonstration of how singularly unique and different it was from any previous document disclosed to the world as part of religious history: first, the emphasis that Bahá-'u'lláh had set the Principles, established the Institutions, and appointed 'Abdu'l-Bahá to interpret His Word for the Bahá'ís; next, the conferring by 'Abdu'l-Bahá upon His grandson, Shoghi Effendi, the necessary authority for the Guardianship; and last, giving to Shoghi Effendi the Plan for an Administrative Order that would guarantee against disintegration or schism of the Faith by any true believer. Nowhere else will one find such important matters as succession and interpretation so clearly spelled out and distinguished from the purely spiritual decrees, in such clear and indisputable language.

In this manner, everything possible to explain had been included in writing for the Bahá'ís: first from Bahá'u'lláh's Covenant, and next from 'Abdu'l-Bahá's Will and Testament, so as to guarantee the preservation of the unity of the obedient followers of the Faith for all time.

Shoghi Effendi's Guardianship had been planned to end one stage and to begin another in the development of the Faith. The first stage included all the steps needed to bring about the birth of the Administrative Order. Now the second one saw the administrative Institutions of the budding Faith begin to take shape in anticipation of the third and final stage, the Golden Age.

Actually, 'Abdu'l-Bahá's preparation for the growth of the New World Order had commenced long before the unveiling of His Will and Testament. Back in 1916–17, He wrote a series of Tablets known as "The Divine Plan," which became later the foundation of the series of steps by which Shoghi Effendi would establish the Administrative Order of the Faith anywhere that it had not yet raised its banner.

The first stage was from 1937 to 1944. It took the form of a teaching campaign for the entire Western Hemisphere, and set the structural basis of the Administrative Order in every state of the United States, every province of Canada, and all of the Republics of Central and South America. It made possible the establishment of the Cause throughout the Western Hemisphere from Anchorage, Alaska, on the north, to Magellanes, Chile, at the southern tip of South America, even including the plan for completion of the exterior of the Bahá'í Temple in Wilmette.

The second stage was from 1946 to 1953. It operated on three continents and covered four main objectives:

The first was the consolidation and further proclamation of the Faith in the United States.

The second was the completion of the interior of the Wilmette edifice.

The third was the formation of three new National Assemblies in the Western Hemisphere—Canada, Central America, and South America. The combined Assembly of the United States and Canada was to be divorced into two separate bodies.

The fourth objective was "the initiation of systematic teaching activity in war-torn, spiritually famished European continent . . . aiming at the establishment of administratively firm, well-grounded Assemblies in the Scandinavian countries, Holland, Belgium, Luxembourg, Switzerland, Italy, and the Iberian Peninsula," all this to be known as the European Teaching Project.

The third part of 'Abdu'l-Bahá's Divine Plan became a Teaching and Consolidation Plan, often referred to as "The World Crusade," which began in 1953 under the Leadership of the Guardian. It saw the establishment of the structure of the Bahá'í Administrative Order in the rest of the world, including Africa, Asia, and the islands of the seas, and terminated with the election of the first Universal House of Justice in 1963.

However, at the time Shoghi Effendi found himself so suddenly made Guardian, this Divine Plan was envisioned only through words set down by 'Abdu'l-Bahá, and the purpose of His Last Will and Testament was to provide the axis around which everything administrative could evolve. Through the Will the Bahá'ís were given the knowledge and understanding written out concisely for them of why the Guardianship and the future Universal House of Justice were divinely ordained, essential in their functions, and complementary in their aim and purpose.

'Abdu'l-Bahá clearly explained why they should be considered as two inseparable pillars to administer the affairs of the Faith, coordinate its activities, promote its interests, execute its laws, and defend its subsidiary institutions. In fact, it was deliberately planned that they would supplement and support each other's authority and functions, by being permanently and fundamentally united in their aims.

The fact that the Guardianship did flourish and that Shoghi Effendi did remain the rock of the Faith for thirty-six years, until the end of his life, proves that 'Abdu'l-Bahá was divinely guided in His choice of a Successor, and that, divorced from the Institution of Guardianship He had set up so perfectly in His Last Will and Testament, the World Order of Bahá'u'lláh might have been destroyed or, at the very least, badly mutilated. Instead, that one example of the divine hereditary principle which has been invariably upheld by the Law of God gave the Bahá'í Faith the guidance and assurance that were needed for gradually defining the sphere of the legislative action of its elected representatives.

Certainly the following words alone from the Will and Testament of 'Abdu'l-Bahá made incontrovertible the fact that Shoghi Effendi was to be considered the continuing interpreter of the Word of God:

> The sacred and youthful branch, the guardian of the Cause of God, as well as the Universal House of Justice to be universally elected and established, are both under the care and protection of the Abha Beauty, under the shelter and unerring guidance of His Holiness, the Exalted One. Whatsoever they decide is of God.

Shoghi Effendi — Bahá'í Guardian, Leader and Husband

SHOGHI EFFENDI was the eldest of five children of his Grandfather's daughter Zia. Interestingly enough, all of 'Abdu'l-Bahá's daughters and their families remained with Him, even after they married, and most of His grandchildren had been born in 'Akká.

Later in Haifa, Shoghi Effendi went to the Jesuit School and afterward to the University of Beirut.

As Shoghi Effendi's widow has written, at the time of 'Abdu'l-Bahá's passing, the future Guardian of the Bahá'í Faith was twenty-four years of age. He was studying at Oxford University in England, because he wanted to learn everything that would help him to be better prepared for his planned dedicated service to his Grandfather in serving as an interpreter and translating some of the Bahá'í literature into English.

"Broken-hearted, so weak from suffering he had to be practically lifted from the train, he returned to Haifa," say the Bahá'í records, which give only a particle of his reaction to his beloved Grandfather's death.

"The second blow," the description continues, "in many ways more cruel than the first, fell upon him . . ." (the knowledge that he was now the Guardian of the Faith). "Saddled with this great weight, crushed by this great blow, he turned his eyes to the Bahá'í world. He beheld a widely diversified, loosely organized community, scattered in various parts of the globe, and with members in about twenty countries. . . .

"We, on our part, beheld a young man of only twenty-four standing at the helm of the Cause and some of the friends felt impelled to advise him about what would be wise for him to do next. It was then that we began to know not only the nature of our Guardian but the nature of the entire Institution of Guardianship, for we quickly discovered that Shoghi Effendi was 'unreachable.' Neither relatives, old Bahá'ís or new Bahá'ís, well-wishers or ill-wishers could sway his judgment or influence his decisions. We quickly came to realize that he was not only divinely guided but he had been endowed by God with just those characteristics needed to build up the Administrative Order, unite the believers in common endeavor, and coordinate their world-wide activities. Shoghi Effendi immediately began to display a genius for organization, for the analysis of problems, for reducing a situation to its component parts and then giving a just and wise solution. He acted vigorously, with unflinching determination and unbounded zeal. Those who were privileged to meet him were immediately captivated by his eager, frank, and cordial attitude, by his consideration, his innate modesty, his spontaneous kindness and charm. The wheels of the Cause which had momentarily stood still at the Master's passing, began to revolve again and at a higher tempo than ever before. He stood our 'true brother,' young, determined to see we at last got down to accomplishing the tasks set us by Bahá'u'lláh and the Master, and not willing to lose any time at all."

When 'Abdu'l-Bahá passed away, the Shrine of the Báb consisted of six rooms, surrounded by a small plot of land. The Mansion of Bahjí and most of its lands were held by those opposed to the Faith, except for the Holy Tomb, itself, in which Bahá'u'lláh was enshrined, and two houses that were for the Bahá'ís visiting from other lands (who were known as pilgrims), but one of these was rented for the Bahá'ís, not owned by them.

Although 'Abdu'l-Bahá was widely loved and respected by those in Palestine (now Israel) He was not considered the Head of a new independent religion, he was considered merely a Great and Holy Man. The young Guardian, with one stroke, severed the bonds that still seemed to tie the Bahá'ís to Islám. He stopped going to the Mosque, and began to accomplish many of the things desired by 'Abdu'l-Bahá.

For a start he added three rooms to the Shrine of the Báb, so that the building would have nine rooms instead of six, as planned by the Master Himself. In 1944, as 'Abdu'l-Bahá had hoped, the model of the completed Shrine was unveiled. It was the occasion of the One Hundredth Anniversary of the Báb's Declaration. The model showed an arcade and a dome, both of which the Master had stated must be included.

By 1953 the actual Shrine was completed, and then the Guardian began gradually to expand the Shrine gardens, designing them personally to the minutest detail. In between he patiently and persistently acquired and bought land for other

Bahá'í gardens, designating the arrangement for each garden and personally supervising all business transactions concerning them.

Through legal means the Mansion at Bahjí was at last restored to the Bahá'ís and was made into a Museum and Holy Place under Shoghi Effendi's supervision. He had all the Bahá'í properties in the Holy Land exempted from government and municipal taxes. He had Bahá'í marriage recognized as legally binding. He secured first from the British and later in much stronger form from the new state of Israel recognition of the World Center of the Faith whose Holy Places are in Haifa and 'Akká and Bahjí, and that he, as Head of this Faith, held a position higher than was held by other merely local or national religious leaders staying in that country.

He selected the design himself and had built monuments over the resting places of the Greatest Holy Leaf, her mother and brother, as well as the wife of 'Abdu'l-Bahá. He likewise detailed exactly how the International Archives building should be set up, approving personally every detail about it, often changing them until they were just the way he desired for the preservation of the precious Bahá'í relics and mementoes such as no previous great religion had ever known.

Shoghi Effendi appealed directly to Israeli government officials and secured Mazra'ih as a Holy Place where the Bahá'í pilgrims could visit, although it was already past the date when the property had been promised to other institutions by the new Jewish State. It was the Guardian who was able to purchase the beautiful Temple site on Mount Carmel, as had been desired by 'Abdu'l-Bahá, and from the World Center Shoghi Effendi sent forth to all continents his own translations, letters, and writings on the Faith in a mighty flow, couched in exquisite language, filled with power, always accurate, profound, and inspired.

From the very beginning of his Guardianship, Shoghi Effendi's was a wise administration and aimed at continually developing his beloved Faith. When 'Abdu'l-Bahá died, there had been few

Bahá'í local spiritual Assemblies in the world, and not even one national Assembly. The Guardian helped the believers throughout the world to direct their efforts through properly organized administrative channels, as indicated by Bahá'u'lláh and defined by 'Abdu'l-Bahá. He made certain that year by year they became more and more free from the bonds of the past, whether those bonds were of close identification with their former religious doctrines and organizations, or the following of the outworn, often corrupt, patterns of conduct alien to the new standards of conduct laid down by the Manifestation of God for the world in this New Day.

Patiently and carefully Shoghi Effendi helped to build strong national institutions for the Faith. He created the International Bahá'í Council, which was the embryonic Universal House of Justice, but kept a balance between something too loosely knit, too individualistic to function effectively, and the overefficiency of too many rules and regulations, as well as too much unnecessary detail which has been one of the great afflictions of present-day civilization.

When the important basics of the Bahá'í Administrative Order were prepared, Shoghi Effendi suddenly shifted the whole mechanism into gear and called for the first Seven-Year Plan, which was his first step in the promulgation of 'Abdu'l-Bahá's Divine Plan. Plan followed plan, as the scattered followers of the Faith began to understand and to work cohesively into the Army of Bahá'u'lláh, guided by their new National Spiritual Assemblies as each was formed. The pioneers, or vanguard, as the Guardian called them, began to march out and into the world until, at the half-way point of the mighty Crusade that had been launched, Shoghi Effendi could look upon a united, strong, enthusiastic, world-wide community of believers in the Faith who had already achieved the major part of the tasks he had set for them in 1953.

From the mind and typewriter of the Guardian poured forth the reams of thoughts and material for the believers, including translations from Bahá'u'lláh's and 'Abdu'l-Bahá's original Words, books of his own messages, his own letters, all done with superlative style and power and frequently supplemented by dynamic cables and special written briefings. Also, at this time, was the creation of his masterful review of the first one hundred years of the greatest Dispensation vouchsafed by God to man on this planet, according to the Bahá'ís, Shoghi Effendi's book *God Passes By*.

He had that vision that could look upon the Cause as a whole, even when it was still a tentative thing of the future. He made certain that whenever possible the precious sites associated wtih the Báb and Bahá'u'lláh and the heroes and martyrs of this Cause were purchased, including the House where Bahá'u'lláh was born in Ṭihrán, His father's house in Tákur, the "black hole" of the Síyáh-Chál where an Angel first told Bahá'u'lláh of His Divine Station, the House He occupied in Constantinople, one of the Houses He occupied in Adrianople, the fortress of Mah-kú where the Báb revealed the Bayán, His shop in Búshihr, and many others. In addition, Shoghi Effendi instructed that an exhaustive photographic record be made and kept of hundreds of these landmarks that were associated with the initial, heroic Age of the Faith.

He stimulated the Persian believers to compile the histories of the early days of the Cause in their own land, and gave the Persian National Spiritual Assembly the great responsibility of collecting and transcribing the Tablets of Bahá'u'lláh and 'Abdu'l-Bahá, thus preserving for posterity a truly priceless heritage.

A builder by nature, the Guardian also oversaw the erection of the House of Worship in America, which will always be unique because its foundation stone had been laid by 'Abdu'l-Bahá Himself. Shoghi Effendi initiated, chose the designs, and set in motion the plans for the erection of the African, the European, the Australasian, the Ṭihrán, and the Holy Land Temples. He specified the sites for the National Headquarters and the national endowments. He named the languages into which the literature of the Faith would be translated, and personally encouraged the pioneers to go forth and fulfill 'Abdu'l-Bahá's Divine Plan.

A believer who worked with Shoghi Effendi wrote later of his manifold efforts:

> Ah, but he did more than this! He made each believer feel that over him watched a just mind and a loving heart; that he had a part to play, was precious to the Faith, had duties to discharge, enjoyed privileges infinitely precious because he was a member of the Community of the Most Great Name. Let us never forget this, never lose sight of this! This oneness he made a reality, this staunch loyalty to our Faith he implanted in our hearts. . . .

But no other individual could ever know him as well as the lady he married.

May Bolles, when she married Sutherland Maxwell in 1902 and went to live in Montreal, was the first Bahá'í in Canada. They visited 'Abdu'l-Bahá as pilgrims in 1909, in the Holy Land, and He later stayed with them when He visited Montreal in 1912. He had shown a special love for their only daughter, Mary, who grew up to be a most active Bahá'í. When Shoghi Effendi became the Guardian, she was already tall, slender, and on fire with love for the Faith, filled with determination to live for it. She spent much time in the United States and helped with the classes at Green Acre many summers. She was privileged to visit the Guardian in Haifa on three different pilgrimages.

What her wedding was like, what her feelings were about her unique husband, these cannot be told by anyone but the former Mary Maxwell, who has been known to the believers as Ruhiyyih Khanum, a name given to her by Shoghi Effendi since the marriage.

At a talk given to the seven thousand Bahá'ís from all over the world in 1963 at Albert Hall, London, England, she described him in minute detail:

> I don't know how anybody could convey the sweetness and the lovableness of the Guardian of the Bahá'í Faith. Many

many people had the privilege of meeting him, but so many others were denied that bounty. . . .

Shoghi Effendi was short in stature. He resembled physically, not so much in his face but very strongly in his body and in his hands, Bahá'u'lláh. The Master was taller. 'Abdu'l-Bahá had blue eyes, but Shoghi Effendi had hazel eyes. I've never seen such expressive eyes in my whole life, never seen eyes that could change so much. Sometimes they were almost golden brown and other times they were absolutely gray and when he was enthusiastic about something he would get so excited that he would open his eyes very wide and you would see the top of the iris. I always thought that these beautiful, beautiful eyes looking at you with such enthusiasm were like two suns rising over the horizon.

He had dark blackish-brown hair. It was, of course, lighter, I believe, when he was a child, but it was at the end quite dark, and he had an olive-skinned complexion. He had exceedingly beautiful hands. . . . They were like what people who study palmistry would say were the hands of an intellectual. They were sensitive and highly developed. . . .

He was the humblest person that I have ever met in my whole life, and I am not just speaking words. . . . He hadn't one speck of personal pride or conceit in his entire make-up. But when it came to the Cause of God he was just like a lion. Insult the Cause, threaten the Cause, offend him as Head of Bahá'u'lláh's Faith and the Sign of God on Earth, and then, believe me, you knew another aspect of Shoghi Effendi!

When he was angry, which he was sometimes, justifiably, his voice was just like the crack of a whip! Nobody could withstand his anger. It was the Wrath of God. . . .

. . . By the time that he did me the great honor of telling me that he had chosen me to be his wife, some of the most difficult days that he had passed through had already gone. He became Guardian in 1921 and he was married in 1937. . . .

When he went away in the summertime, he used to set aside practically up to the very last years of his life, a budget for himself and whoever was with him had to live on that budget also. He always, of course, was accompanied by somebody, one of his relatives or his secretary. . . . Whether it was two people or seven people, the budget had to suffice.

When I was first married and went away with the Beloved Guardian, he took me to places that, although Mary Maxwell's family hadn't been very wealthy, I had never stayed in during my life—such modest places. Shoghi Effendi used to travel— in fact, we both did— third class, and third-class seats have progressed nowadays, but before World War II they were usually of wood and they were very hard. And, if he had any traveling to do overnight, he used to put his rucksack or whatever it was, roll up his coat, put it under his head and go to sleep. Although those accompanying him were all as young or younger than the Guardian, and fairly tough young men, they couldn't stand it, they would get absolutely worn out and they couldn't understand how Shoghi Effendi could sleep all night long just on something rolled under his head, just rolled up on a wooden bench.

He loved mountaineering and used to go for these long, long walks, after he first became Guardian, in the mountains. He climbed some high mountains in Switzerland, but mostly he used to go on walks, not the actual alpine climbs. Although he used to go on some with guides and parties and ropes and so on. He loved it. He seemed to find a great comfort from the mountains, even up to the end of his life. . . .

One of the strongest characteristics of the Guardian was his absolutely iron principle that *nothing* could interfere with what he considered right. Nothing swayed him at all. Neither love nor hate nor danger—absolutely nothing. . . . If there was a matter of principle involved, the principle applied to everyone exactly the same. It was these examples of Shoghi Effendi's diamond-like integrity that strengthened and sustained so many tests in Haifa. . . .This kind of integrity will keep the Cause spotless for a thousand years. It's the kind of integrity that *all* the Bahá'ís must follow, and the integrity that all the Assemblies must follow, because it is the Standard of God!

Once we had in Haifa a Bahá'í whose husband was a Catholic. They were touring the world and she asked permission to come there. She was a devoted Bahá'í and wanted to know if her husband could come with her, and much to my surprise, because I had a little, limited mind, not a *great* mind like Shoghi Effendi, he said "Yes." So we had this Bahá'í and her Catholic husband who, of course, had been in contact with the Faith for years, but had not become a Bahá'í at all, at the Pilgrim House table. The Guardian was so kind to that man, such a perfect host to him. He subjugated all the purely sort of family Bahá'í kind of conversation to topics that might be of interest to this non-Bahá'í. You see, that perfect courtesy and consideration, that desire to make the *non*-Bahá'í feel at home and attracted and happy. It was so wonderfully exemplified by Shoghi Effendi. . . .

I'd like to tell you the story of the developments of the Holy Places in all their beauty as you see them now. You know, Shoghi Effendi was born a prisoner and he wasn't released from imprisonment—at least, *technical* imprisonment in the City of 'Akká until he was twelve years old. And he never had any opportunity to come in contact with culture as we know it in the West. He was not brought up in a home that had any decoration in it whatsoever. Remember how bare and simple the Home of 'Abdu'l-Bahá was, and all of those places in the early days were. It wasn't until just before the last war that the Guardian began to beautify the premises, and the reason he did it was two things. First of all, the Cause was growing all the time, having more prestige, more fame, and second, it gradually had more money.

I heard that Bahá'u'lláh had a little tiny chest in His room in the Mansion in Bahjí, and in it He had all the money of the Bahá'í Faith. And He used to open it and take out a few gold pieces or silver pieces and pay the expenses of the house and the community. 'Abdu'l-Bahá in His days had a banking account. The Master had more money, and then Shoghi Effendi had a little bit more. As the years went by he had more to spend on the Cause, and because of that he said that now the time had come when it was proper to make the Shrines as beautiful as possible and also to embellish the other Holy Places. . . .

In 1940, during the darkest days of the War, the beloved Guardian, my father, and I were here in London, and it was at that time that he ordered some of the first vases for the shrines . . . these Greek-style marble urns, and they were delivered to us later on. . . .

. . . I remember Shoghi Effendi used to design all the paths of the gardens, even to where the trees were to be planted and the flower beds, and he used to tell the gardener, "Measure it out in spans," and the gardener would go along and then he would plant a cypress tree and he would measure more spans and he'd plant another cypress tree and so on. The whole thing came from Shoghi Effendi.

But sometimes we had very difficult technical problems such as building staircases . . . and I would try and make him little paper models. . . . Finally my father turned up because, after my mother's passing, Shoghi Effendi, with that beautiful spirit of gentleness and love he had, came to me and said, "Now that your mother is dead your father's place is here with us," and he sent for him. . . . But, anyway, he was going to build a flight of stairs and I said, "Shoghi Effendi, why do you bother anymore? You have a very good Canadian architect just waiting—tell him what you want and you'll have it."

And I remember those beautiful eyes just looked at me and got so round and he said, "Can he do it?" and I said, "Why, this is a joke for him, this is child's play." So Shoghi Effendi told my father what he wanted, and he built the first stairs and from then on it was a very, very precious association, because this was something my father *could* do, and it resulted, of course, in the end, in the construction of the Shrine of the Báb.

But you must know, even *that* building had Shoghi Effendi's touch throughout, because he told Daddy it must be an arcade at the bottom, because that was what the Master said, it must have a dome, it must have a clerestory section in between, and when he built those things on the clerestory—they're like minarets sticking up—Shoghi Effendi didn't like the original design, and I can't tell you how many drawings my father made and brought over for the Guardian, until finally there was a design that Shoghi Effendi liked and he said, "Yes, now the proportion is right, this is the way I want it."

And my father considered that the Guardian, apart from *being* the Guardian, was a man of exceptional taste and exceptional sense of proportion. Everything that the Guardian did, you see that extraordinary sense of proportion, and, of course, proportion *is* beauty and proportion is part of order.

When the Guardian used to go out, sometimes he would find me very impatiently waiting for him to get in the car and go up to the Shrines.

He'd say, "I know—you want to go up and clean your room," and I'd say, "Yes. . . ."

So, when he went, I would immediately get busy with the girls and we would clean *his* room first, because, of course, we couldn't do it when he was there. He had a great many things on his desk. He had two pen holders here, one on either side, and he had a picture of the interior of the Shrine of Bahá'u'lláh and he had blotting paper and a box with stationery and letters in it, quite a lot of things, not anything like a big American executive's desk. So, when he came back, quite unconsciously he would come around behind his desk and he'd just go like that! Just touching with his fingertips, one little twist, until he had every single thing within a milli-meter of where it had been when he went out. It was the most extraordinary thing, and of course we'd worked so hard to get everything back to where it was in the first place! But it was most typical of him—this *marvelous* sense of order. . . .

. . . He wasn't often ill during the period I was with him, but one time he had sand fever and a temperature of over 104 and he didn't want to go to Haifa this way. This was at the outbreak of war, we had just arrived back in Palestine, and just, incidentally, gotten safely out of Europe, and he said, "If I go to Haifa and it is known that I am ill, the rumor will go back to Persia and it will distress the hearts of the Persian Bahá'ís and when it reaches the villagers it may be exag-gerated and it will cause them suffering and I don't want them to be distressed. . . ."

So we went away to a small place and his mother came and his secretary used to come every day and bring the mail from Haifa, but nobody else knew that he had returned to Palestine. And this cable was brought, saying that Martha Root had died in Honolulu. And this Blessed Guardian of ours, with his face so wan and so pale and so weak, began to pull himself up in his bed on his pillows, to sit up.

I said, "Shoghi Effendi, you *mustn't* sit up, it's dangerous! You have a very high fever!"

And he said, "No! I have to! I have to answer this cable!"

But I said, "Shoghi Effendi, the cable will have to wait! You are very ill. You mustn't make such an effort at a time like this!"

He said, "Don't you understand? The greatest teacher in the Bahá'í World has died and they are waiting to hear what I am going to say about her. It *can't* wait!"

And under those circumstances he dictated that marvelous cable of tribute to Martha Root. And then he fell back in bed, absolutely exhausted, and went on being ill.

He used to say, "Do you realize that I can never have a moment's respite?" He said, "A bank president, a president of a country, a king, a prime minister, anybody can go away and delegate their powers to someone else for a short time, but I can't hand this Cause over to anyone for a single instant."

No matter what condition Shoghi Effendi was in, he had to go on every moment of his life, until his heart stopped, being the Guardian of the Bahá'í Faith and carrying this terrible burden that 'Abdu'l-Bahá's Will placed on his shoulders. . . .

Few people realized how much the former Mary Maxwell— Ruhíyyih Khánum—shared the burdens that the Guardian had, from the moment they married. And yet even she was prevented from interfering in what he felt were his responsibilities. She might *suggest*, but she could never *decide* for him.

Her destiny seemed to have given her a special character, strength, and understanding, from the time of her childhood. After a life of comparative luxury and independence with her mother and father, it must have been quite an internal battle for an independent, self-willed Western woman to be able to conform to all the rules of life with a family of the purely Eastern background.

Even today, Ruhíyyih Khánum insists on saying she is not remotely photogenic, but her friends see in her a rare spiritual beauty emphasized by high cheek bones, a tall, lithe body and excellent carriage, a lack of self-interest, and a knowledge of how to make the most of any circumstances which may confront her. Her light brown hair is worn simply; always it is covered outdoors by a scarf or a turban, as is considered modest and correct for a lady of her rank in Eastern circles, but her opinions are given frankly, courteously, and concisely. She is warm and human and kindly, interested in everything and everyone, and like the Guardian does not want to be "protected" from life, regardless of how hard or cruel or disappointing it may become.

In 1951, when the Guardian called some of the believers to Haifa to help him, they suddenly realized the burden he had been under. His face was often sad, and one could recognize that his very spirit must have been heavily oppressed many times. He had a profound and innate humility and was so self-effacing that he would brush aside adulation and praise or turn any kind words showered upon him by the believers toward the Central Figures of the Faith. They noticed that he would never allow any photographs to be taken of himself, or give any of himself, but invariably encouraged the friends to place 'Abdu'l-Bahá's picture in their rooms. Nor would he permit anyone to have his discarded clothes or personal possessions, because he did not want these to be regarded as relics either. Indeed, he disliked very much any obvious signs of personal worship toward himself. For some reason, however, he did permit one of the Bahá'ís to take a few snapshots of him on the last day he was ever to be in Haifa, and from these have been selected some special ones that are being shared with the Bahá'ís everywhere, in the volume of the "Bahá'í World" telling of his life and death.

Back in the middle 1930s, however, when close friends of the Maxwells suggested to young Mary the possibility that she might become the wife of the Guardian, she was honestly shocked and considered such a thought as heresy. You may well imagine how overwhelmed she was in Haifa when Shoghi Effendi did tell her that he had chosen her to be his wife.

"When the day of our marriage came," she told the friends at the London Congress, "I was dressed entirely in black, because in those days they wore black whenever the ladies went out on the street in the East. I had a black turban on my head and black shoes and a black bag and a black suit and black gloves. I had on a white blouse, I admit, but that was my wedding outfit.

"I came over to the Master's House—I'd been frightfully cross to my parents all morning, because I was so terribly, terribly nervous. Most people only get married once, but not everybody gets married to a Guardian. So, I would alternately get cross with my parents, then throw my arms around their necks and weep and beg forgiveness all morning.

"By the time the afternoon came, I went over and the beloved Guardian came out and got into his car. I got in beside him, and the heavens fell in Haifa, because no one had wind of this. They were all simply astonished at the Guardian, since going off in an automobile with a Western Bahá'í woman was simply unheard of. . . . We went over to the Shrine of Bahá'u'lláh and prayed and this ring that I wear was Shoghi Effendi's Bahá'í ring. It was given to him by the Greatest Holy Leaf and he had always worn it on this finger and he was, of course, very attached to it. So, the day that he told me that he had chosen me for this great honor, he put this ring on my finger. But then he said—'Now, no one must see that you are wearing it,' so I took it off and wore it around my neck on a chain until the day we went to the Shrine of Bahá'u'lláh. And then we just had prayers in the Shrine, and he put the ring on my finger. That was all. Silently. It was no place for conversation. And he went inside the inner shrine and gathered up all the dried flowers that were there and he took the flowers and gave them to my mother that night as a gift.

"And we went back and in the room of the Greatest Holy Leaf we had this simple ceremony of Bahá'u'lláh—putting hand in hand, and I recited a verse which I had learned with great difficulty in Arabic and he recited it and that was all! Then I think we went over and sat with his family for a few moments, and I finally went back to the pilgrim house and waited for him to come over for dinner just as he always did—we sat with my mother and father, and I was there with his brother, just like we did every other night, and dear Fujita waiting on him, and then after dinner my luggage was carried across the street upstairs.

"We went and sat and visited for some time in a room with his parents and brothers and sisters, and that was our marriage. Just as simple as that. No wedding veil, no special flowers, no long Tablets chanted, nothing. . . . It seemed to me very wonderful and very precious. So you see, when one of our Bahá'ís said the other day, 'The Bahá'í Faith is simple,' I think he had the right idea. . . .

"I had a room next to his bedroom which was also his working room. He had his bed and his desk side by side, because he used to work until he was *so* exhaused that he just *fell* into bed, and then he would go on working in his bed. And *nothing* I did could get Shoghi Effendi to separate his bedroom from his office. He just wouldn't.

"He said, 'I can't help it, it's all in one place, and I can get into bed and out of bed and do my work and it's impossible.' And he went right on to the end of his life, his bed and his desk side by side."

An American Bahá'í, who visited with the Guardian in 1937, reported details of this experience:

We met every morning after breakfast in the workshop of Shoghi Effendi, on the top of the large house occupied by 'Abdu'l-Bahá during the last years of his life. Usually Shoghi Effendi had already read his mail when I saw him and he would ask one or the other to answer certain letters, which, when returned to him, were either approved or amended. Here is the center of our planet socially speaking. Papers will be on file concerning world matters in this center not heretofore possible.

Shoghi Effendi works mercilessly, regardless of sleep, meals, etc., and it is the constant wish of the family to get him to take reasonable exercise in the open air. He sometimes took walks which were devoted to serious talks and just as in the study, all his waking hours are given to severe mental labor. . . . He handles problems arising with a sincerity, force, and decision that brings joy to everyone and in his remarkable letters brings results to us here. His executive ability is marvelous. The East and the West are curiously united in him. His mind and methods are western and his spirit has that subtle profundity which is the inheritance of the East with all the spiritual thought. His power, energy, and decision is one of the most impressive things of all, and when a decision is made his unswerving policy is very inspiring and gratifying. . . . Gibraltar is a shifting sand compared with the mind of Shoghi Effendi when made up. . . .

It is interesting to compare this account of the Guardian's working habits with one written by a Bahá'í in the early part of this century who had observed how 'Abdu'l-Bahá worked:

His correspondence is carried on in a large room in the lower story where five or six stenographers await him. [He] seldom dictates one letter at a time. As a rule, his stenographers sit in a line. He begins at one end with the paragraph of a letter destined perhaps for America, pauses at the next, and begins one for Persia, pauses again with some words for a believer in Turkey, and so on down the succession of busy paragraphers. More surprising than all he frequently carries on a lively conversation while in the act of dictating. . . . The dictation is always in the Oriental languages of the individuals to whom the tablets are addressed, and ʻAbduʼl-Bahá will spring from Turkish to Aramaic, then into Persian or Arabic without an instant's hesitation, but if he is sending to a Western country, he speaks in swift Persian and the stenographer translates the epistle, which reaches its consignee in both languages.

. . . Each one is so psychologically attuned to the person to whom it is written that it would seem as if it could only be indited by someone familiar with every detail of the recipient's life and soul. Yet, in all probability, ʻAbduʼl-Bahá has received merely a formal expression of faith from His correspondent. . . . On the morning it was answered, ʻAbduʼl-Bahá took it out from the mass of papers and dispatched His reply because He felt that the psychologic moment had arrived when the stranger so far away needed the vital touch of His dynamic spirit. . . .

During her marriage to the Guardian, Ruḥíyyih Khánum was for sixteen of the twenty years his secretary. When they were away from Haifa, she performed the work done by others for him at home, such as attending to the details of mail, callers, etc., as well as being his companion.

When there was good news to impart to the friends, there was no one as joyous as Shoghi Effendi himself.

"He couldn't *wait* to send out the news," his widow recalls again and again. "He used to cable the National Spiritual Assembly of Central and East Africa and ask them, 'How many have you now?' so that he could put it in his next message [to the Baháʼí World].

"He used to come with a shining face to the pilgrims—Persian and Western—and couldn't wait to tell them, 'Do you know that there are now six thousand to ten thousand—or whatever it was

—Bahá'ís in Central and East Africa, and that there are so-and-so many more Bahá'ís in this country and that country or the other country?'

"At times I used to *long* to close the door, to not allow anything to get at him, and yet I didn't *dare* do it. . . . And so I remember I had to wake him in the middle of the night and tell him that his mother had just died of a heart attack.

"I had to go into his room and whisper—he was asleep—'Shoghi Effendi, Shoghi Effendi,' and he woke and then gradually as best I could, because she had to be buried the next morning, he was told finally that his mother had just died. . . .

"Another thing that illumined my mind very much in relation to Shoghi Effendi was something that our dear friends from Central and East Africa will remember. He heard that there was a Bahá'í in Kitali Prison for murder . . . and that this Bahá'í was teaching other Bahá'ís and some of the prisoners accepted the Cause. . . . He cabled the Bahá'í World in one of his messages and mentioned the prisoners in Kitali.

"This was such a revelation to me. I had thought it was a terrible disgrace, that we should try to hide the fact that there was such a thing as a Bahá'í in prison and here he was telling the other Bahá'ís that Bahá'ís have been given the right to celebrate their Holy Days in Kitali Prison and he wrote to them in Kitali Prison and encouraged them! So you see, all these things teach us . . . there is room for practically everyone in the Bahá'í Faith. . . ."

In a letter to her mother, which Mrs. Maxwell had shared with some of the friends, Ruhíyyih Khanum wrote of her husband:

> If anyone should ask me what my theme in life was I should say "Shoghi Effendi." I not only feel absorbed in him (I do not mean for a moment as a wife in a husband), but feel that I want to be more absorbed in him and that in that way lies all my salvation. . . . He is fair to a degree that is like a mathematical instrument, a scales. He never misjudges even an enemy; he is justice embodied. And when we do not deserve his love, I sometimes think we just don't get it. . . . It is this wonderful justice—so heavy on our hands when we seek

mercy, forgiveness, and comforting love—that is the hope of life for all. . . . Love, today, I feel, is of very little use to mankind. It won't right wrongs, it won't shield the abused or feed the multitudes, all it does is to make the individual warm and comforted, but justice will stand by every man, protect him, discipline him, make him strong, and give him legitimate dues in life. From each other and God we receive love—and this justice is a form of love and bounty to us. . . .

To get back to the subject of the Guardian, I sometimes think that he administers his justice with a degree of patience, long suffering, and forbearance that we do not dream of. If I can say it, I feel that he endures anything that can only harm *him* and *his* feelings, but if it harm the Cause, its honor or interest, then he will not tolerate it at all. And if the believers knew how he suffered, how bitter the cup he often drinks from, they would love him with a consuming, weeping tenderness and devotion—as so many of them do. He is so golden-hearted, so pure-hearted, that sometimes when I catch a glimpse of it I am stunned.

Only a short while before the world was to learn that the Guardian who had worked so hard for thirty-six years would never suffer again, weep again, or work again, Mrs. Florence Mayberry, an American believer, had the memorable experience of meeting Shoghi Effendi during her Haifa pilgrimage. At the 1965 National Convention of the Bahá'ís of the United States she shared a few of her recollections of him at the Shrine of the Báb:

. . . Shoghi Effendi walked around to the other side with the men. The ladies walked in the opposite room with Rúhíyyih Khánum. Each according to his desire kneeled or stood to say prayers.

After a while there was the most beautiful, the most glorious, the most lyrical voice I have heard in my life and it began to chant. In that voice was the poignancy of the Prophet of God Who came only to help the world and the people of the world were blinded by passion, by ignorance, by obstinacy. . . . The poignancy was for the poor limited suffering of mankind. The voice of the Guardian lifted and lifted and lifted. It seemed to go through the dome of the Shrine right into the heavens. . . .

... There's good reason for me to say that perhaps the most important thing I will have to do in the next World of God is to tell them, "Yes, I was there in the Holy Land; I heard the Sweet Singer of God—the Guardian. . . ."

Those who were privileged to know Shoghi Effendi from the time of his childhood until his passing remember him as being incarnate with life; a dynamic, almost electric force, always busy, restless, intense in all aspects of his nature, with phenomenal powers of concentration and accomplishment. That the Bahá'í Faith in 1957 had reached so vital and conclusive a point that it could proceed without him physically is proven by its continuing to grow since his passing that year at the age of sixty-one.

The fact that he did everything important himself, personally, not only was for him to make certain it was done right, but to make it possible to save the Cause large sums of money and, in effect, to thus go on with new enterprises by using the money saved from something else. For thirty-six years Shoghi Effendi held in his hands the funds of the Faith at its World Center, and nothing was done or paid out without his personal approval and consideration. It was the Guardian who, entirely aside from the glorious spiritual leadership manifested in his letters, his books, and his words to the pilgrims, so harbored the financial resources of the Faith that during his lifetime many splendid goals became reality, many, many lasting landmarks were finished or created, and so very many plans were able to be started on their way.

On October 20, 1957, he and Ruhiyyih Khanum arrived in London to finish selecting the furniture and other items needed for the interior of the International Archives Building and the Gardens above it. Shoghi Effendi had chosen London for this purpose because it is an international center where items from every country abound and cost less than probably anywhere else in the world. As was his custom during any absence from Haifa, no contact was made with any Bahá'í. Ruhiyyih Khanum helped him as she always did.

That Sunday afternoon, October 27, he spoke of stiffness and pain in his hands, and said that he was "so tired, so tired." That night he had a fever and by the following day it was so high that a doctor was called in. Both the Guardian and his wife had the Asiatic flu, but Shoghi Effendi's was more severe due to his always having worked too hard, which had resulted in a high blood pressure condition for a number of years. Despite his family and his personal physician in Haifa having pleaded constantly that he not overdo so much, he had continued his routine of spending hours each afternoon and evening with the visiting pilgrims, after having risen early in the morning to do all that had to be done by the one person who could make decisions for this rapidly growing Faith.

He was known to go to the Gardens in all types of weather directing the various projects there. Or he would do the same with the Holy Places planned on Mount Carmel or at Bahjí. If he had some deep problem or anguish he could not eat for days and for weeks before this last illness he admittedly had no appetite.

Shoghi Effendi was more concerned for the bronchitis Ruhíyyih Khanum developed after the "flu" than for his own continuing illness. Instead of taking more than a few days to get completely well, within a short time he insisted on personally going over his mail and answering it or doing other work while sitting up in bed. It did no good for the doctor to insist the patient do nothing. He rested only occasionally, getting up to obtain papers from the desk, exerting himself unduly, even on the days when his temperature rose alarmingly.

That Saturday morning he told his wife to place a table in the room large enough so that he could lay on it the map of the Bahá'í World on which he had been working, which showed the progress of the Bahá'í work. It was called "The Half-Way Point of the Ten-Year Crusade," and despite her pleas, Shoghi Effendi insisted on completing the map and worked steadily on it for about three hours.

Although he looked tired afterwards, he continued reading reports he had received, while lying back in bed. That evening he explained to Ruhíyyih Khanum some of the work he was going to do on Mount Carmel, how he going to finish the International Archives Building with the things that had been ordered, and remarked on a number of other things. Long afterwards Ruhiyyih Khanum mentioned to some of the believers in Haifa that at the time she couldn't understand his reasons for being so explicit, but that somehow all of his words and instructions and wishes had remained fixed in her mind.

The Guardian continued to work all the next day, and since it was a Sunday he decided the doctor should have some rest. When the physician telephoned, Shoghi Effendi relayed the message through his wife that he felt better and that there would be no need of the medical visit.

He and Ruhiyyih Khanum spent a happy evening talking together. At ten o'clock she made the Guardian comfortable, then left the room so he could sleep, first asking that he be sure to call her if he required anything during the night.

The next morning was Monday, November 4. Ruhiyyih Khanum had slept badly all night, and with her heart feeling heavy and sad she knocked on the door of the Guardian's room and, when there was no answer, entered.

She thought he was still asleep, or possibly drowsily half-awake, and she asked him how he had slept and if he felt better. When he neither moved nor answered and seemed so unnaturally still, a wave of agonizing terror swept over her. She reached out to seize his hand. Although he was absolutely rigid when the doctor arrived, to pacify the Guardian's frenzied wife he gave Shoghi Effendi heart injections and massaged his heart, but all, of course, to no avail. Nothing in the world could have helped because a clot of blood that suddenly entered into one of the heart vessels was the cause of death.

Ruhiyyih Khanum and the other believers were grateful for one thing. Their dearly beloved Guardian, the sacred and so dearly loved Trust left to them by 'Abdu'l-Bahá, had passed away peacefully with no pain. His eyes bore no look of surprise, although they were open.

It is said that such deaths are reserved for the just.

The International
Aspects of the Faith

The Last Rites for Shoghi Effendi

ALTHOUGH Ruhiyyih Khanum, widow of Shoghi Effendi Rabbani, Guardian of the Bahá'í Faith, has always avoided personal disclosures about herself, it must be noted here that by her marriage to Shoghi Effendi in 1937, as an American-born individual living in Canada during her youth, she represented to the rapidly expanding Bahá'í community the height of distinction and loyalty. She was regarded then, and still is now, as someone special who brought to the Faith and its Guardian an exemplary devotion.

Her services are still remembered as a member of the first American Bahá'í Youth Committee, as a Bahá'í teacher, and the moving power with which she frequently spoke about the early martyrs of the Faith in Bahá'í summer schools and other places. Her travels in Europe, her Bahá'í teaching there, especially her superb teaching work in Germany, had aroused warm admiration and concern for her.

When she married the Guardian, the American and Canadian believers in particular felt they had an additional tie binding them not only to each other but to the Institution of the Guardianship. The marriage was a symbol of the union of the East and West and in her new life the former Mary Maxwell was

to achieve knowledge, standards, and memories unique to someone reared in the Western traditions.

Bahá'ís everywhere grieved with Ruhíyyih Khanum when,
"half-mad with grief," as she has described herself, immediately
after the passing of Shoghi Effendi she had to find the strength
within herself to gather near her those few close friends called
Hands of the Cause of God, to assist in the funeral preparations
while she personally conveyed to the Bahá'í World the tragic
and unexpected news. It was in a special cable that they learned
of his death, and that already there had come to an end another
remarkable era in the history of the Faith of Bahá'u'lláh:

SHOGHI EFFENDI BELOVED ALL HEARTS SACRED TRUST GIVEN
BELIEVERS BY MASTER PASSED AWAY SUDDENLY HEART ATTACK
IN SLEEP FOLLOWING ASIATIC FLU. URGE BELIEVERS REMAIN
STEADFAST, CLING INSTITUTION HANDS LOVINGLY REARED, RE-
CENTLY REINFORCED, EMPHASIZED BY BELOVED GUARDIAN,
ONLY ONENESS OF HEART ONENESS OF PURPOSE CAN BEFIT-
TINGLY TESTIFY LOYALTY ALL NATIONAL ASSEMBLIES AND
BELIEVERS TO DEPARTED GUARDIAN WHO SACRIFICED SELF
UTTERLY FOR SERVICE FAITH. RUHIYYIH.

In a second message cabled the same day, November 5, 1957,
Ruhíyyih Khanum added: APPEAL HANDS, NATIONAL ASSEM-
BLIES AUXILIARY BOARDS TO SHELTER BELIEVERS ASSIST THEM
MEET HEART-RENDING, SUPREME TEST. FUNERAL OUR BE-
LOVED SATURDAY NINTH LONDON. HANDS, ASSEMBLY BOARD
MEMBERS INVITED ATTEND. . . . URGE HOLD MEMORIAL MEET-
INGS SATURDAY.

On Sunday, November 10, the National and Regional Spiritual Assemblies received this message from Ruhíyyih Khanum,
which was written after the funeral services in London had been
held:

BELOVED GUARDIAN LAID REST LONDON ACCORDING LAWS
AQDAS BEAUTIFUL BEFITTING SPOT AFTER IMPRESSIVE CERE-
MONY HELD PRESENCE MULTITUDE BELIEVERS REPRESENTING
OVER TWENTY COUNTRIES EAST WEST STOP DOCTORS AS-

SURE SUDDEN PASSING INVOLVED NO SUFFERING. BLESSED COUNTENANCE BORE EXPRESSION INFINITE BEAUTY, PEACE, MAJESTY STOP. EIGHTEEN HANDS ASSEMBLED FUNERAL URGE NATIONAL BODIES REQUEST ALL BELIEVERS HOLD MEMORIAL MEETINGS EIGHTEENTH NOVEMBER COMMEMORATING DAY-SPRING DIVINE GUIDANCE WHO HAS LEFT US AFTER THIRTY-SIX YEARS UTTER SELF-SACRIFICE, CEASELESS LABORS CONSTANT VIGILANCE.

Then, on the following day, November 12, this further cable-gram was received by the administrative centers of the Baha'í World from Ruhiyyih Khanum:

ASSURE FRIENDS BELOVED, SACRED GUARDIAN BEFITTINGLY LAID REST SURROUNDED BY LARGE, REPRESENTATIVE GATHER-ING BELIEVERS EAST WEST. LIGHT OUR LIVES DEPARTED, WE MUST NOW STAND FIRM, REMEMBERING PEERLESS EXAMPLE HIS DEDICATION WORK BLESSED PERFECTION, GLORIOUS VIC-TORIES HE WON, PLANS HE LONGED SEE COMPLETED, ONLY REDEDICATION, GREATER UNITY, STEADFAST SERVICE CAN BE-FITTINGLY SHOW OUR GRIEF MAKE US ACCEPTABLE HOLY THRESHOLD. RUHIYYIH.

Between the passing of the Guardian and the sending of these cables, Ruhiyyih Khanum demonstrated a strength and nobility of spirit, in addition to unique bravery that she has shown and maintained upon many other public occasions since then.

Drawing upon the group of Hands of the Cause of God, of which she was a member, Ruhiyyih Khanum turned to two in Britain, one in Rome, and one in the Holy Land to join her as soon as they could. In order to advise Haifa gently of the terrible loss the Baha'ís had suffered, she merely cabled there in the morning to advise the believers that he was desperately ill. How-ever, this cable arrived *after* the one she sent in the afternoon giving the dread news of the Guardian's passing, and it was broadcasts of their irreconcilable loss that were heard by many Baha'ís throughout the universe, without any prior warning of the blow to come.

The customs in the West are different from those in the East. Very careful instructions had to be given to the undertaker in London, to explain that in the Bahá'í religion there is no embalmment, that no injections of any kind must be used to preserve the body (unless necessitated by law), and that the Bahá'ís would arrange to wash the body themselves.

The believers had to bear in mind that in all the funeral arrangements to be made, the Laws which the Guardian had so repeatedly stressed and constantly upheld had to be remembered and obeyed. The size of London and the fact that the only available burial grounds lie in its outskirts, had also to be remembered, so that no mistake would be made in transporting the Guardian's precious remains more than an hour's journey, this being a Bahá'í provision for special reasons.

It was the longing of the Hands helping Ruhiyyih Khanum, who were then responsible for all the pressing matters that had to be attended to in such a short space of time, to have him transported to the National Bahá'í Building in London, where the believers could gather and pray until the time of the funeral. Investigation, however, showed that it would take more than an hour to go there and then to the cemetery, so that idea was discarded.

One of the Hands from Germany was requested by Ruhiyyih Khanum to wash the body, since he was a physician and would not only be able to endure the sorrow of performing this act, but as a very spiritual person would also do it in the spirit of consecration and prayer required on such a sacred occasion.

Due to the delays and the many arrangements that had to be made, the funeral was set for noon on Saturday, November 9. It was hoped to secure a piece of land especially for burial, but English law restricted the use of land near London for this purpose. Under Bahá'í Law the grave site had to be within an hour's journey from where the body lay. The first place they looked at was dreary and depressing, despite being near many pretentious vaults.

The second place, however, was perfect. It was twilight when they entered a beautiful, peaceful spot on a hill, surrounded by rolling country, where birds sang in the trees, and the woods of the countryside lay close to it on one side. It was the highest part of the cemetery, right in the center, and it adjoined one of the roads, while bounded by three great trees which cast their shade over it. It was over thirty meters square, and Ruhíyyih Khánum arranged to purchase it immediately, and gave instructions to build a deep, strong vault.

The Hands, including a second member from Germany who had arrived, proceeded to the undertaker's where they chose a lead coffin that could be hermetically sealed, and a beautiful casket in which it could be placed. By so doing, the Hands were assured that in the future, when the means of transport might have become so rapid that the journey from London to Haifa would take only one hour, the sacred remains of the Guardian could be taken to the Holy Land for reburial there, should this be desired.

By this time, other dignitaries of the Faith had arrived from all over the world. Ruhíyyih Khánum was joined by a very dear friend, also a Hand of the Cause, Mrs. Amelia Collins, who gave her much-needed motherly love and support.

After the Guardian's body had been washed by Dr. Adelbert Muhlschlegel, the Hand from Germany who had been permitted this special task that Thursday, Ruhíyyih Khánum asked to be alone with her beloved husband to say her own last farewell. Whatever her feelings at that time, they were too private and precious to be discussed, although she did remark to the Bahá'ís later:

> He was our Guardian, King of the world. We know he was noble because he was our Guardian. We know that God gave him peace in the end. But as I looked at him all I could think of was—how beautiful he is, how beautiful! A celestial beauty seemed to be poured over him and to rest on him and to stream from him like a mighty benediction from on high. And the wonderful hands, so like the hands of Bahá'u'lláh, lay

softly by his side; it seemed impossible the life had gone from them—or that radiant face.

After the coffin was closed, a green pall was spread over it, and a large sheath of red roses, epecially supervised and chosen by Ruhiyyih Khanum, was placed on the top.

It is interesting to note how all the non-Bahá'ís concerned with the death and burial of this special stranger who had passed away in their country so suddenly were deeply touched and stirred by the great reverence and love that accompanied the still form of God's Great Guardian as he passed from life to the grave. They outdid themselves in offering sympathy and cooperation.

At the four corners of the grave the florist had already planted four beautiful small cypress trees ordered by Ruhiyyih Khanum in memory of the hundreds of such trees planted by Shoghi Effendi during his lifetime. At the top of the Chapel, which was entirely nondenominational and used for services of all religions, was an arched alcove filled with a bank of chrysanthemums and asters, beginning with deep shades of purple and running up through violet, lavender, and orchid tones to white at the top. Like two arms reaching out, garlands of lavender chrysanthemums ran along a cornice which framed the raised upper part of the Chapel.

Above this, wall-to-wall, was a beam of wood, in the center of which was hung the Bahá'í Holy Symbol, a framed Greatest Name. Beneath this, in front of the alcove of flowers, the coffin rested on a low catafalque covered by a rich green velvet pall, the color to which the descendants of Muhammad are entitled by their illustrious lineage, and which the Guardian, as a Siyyid himself, through his kinship to the Báb, had every right to bear with him to the grave. Seating arrangements placed the Hands of the Cause on the right and on the left side of the coffin facing it, and a hundred more chairs than usually needed in the Chapel were ordered.

The spontaneous gesture of esteem from the Israeli Government, requesting that their Chargé d'Affaires at the Israeli Embassy be permitted to attend the funeral on behalf of the government (the Ambassador being absent from his post) was graciously accepted. Even though it had been planned to have the services entirely private, he was probably the only non-Bahá'í permitted on this occasion.

A ceaseless flow of cables, telephone calls from all parts of the globe, and innumerable Press inquiries and releases over the wires, made it plain that a great wave of love, sorrow, and interest was developing about the loss of the Guardian. It became obvious that the funeral would be attended by many more of the Bahá'ís than it had been thought could reach London in time since not only were the Bahá'ís of Great Britain attending practically en masse, but so were the Hands of the Cause, various members from National Assemblies both near and far, Auxiliary Board members, and individual believers pouring in from overseas.

More than sixty automobiles, filled with over three hundred and sixty people, moved in solemn file to where they were joined by the hearse bearing the coffin. This was preceded by a floral hearse and followed by the car containing the widow, and the other cars. It was probably the largest column of funeral vehicles seen in London for many years for a personage of any denomination. The cortege proceeded to the Great Northern London Cemetery at New Southgate.

When the service started, the Chapel was overflowing and many Bahá'ís had to remain outside during the special prayers and reading of selections from the Bahá'í Writings. Those who were part of the service had beautiful voices. The words were in Persian, Arabic, or English, and the believers present were representative of Bahá'ís from Europe, Asia, Africa, America— highly diverse religious and ethnic groups.

At the grave site, the flowers were removed from the casket to show the beautifully engraved tablet on the cover.

Graciously, knowing the need of the friends to say a brief

personal farewell to their beloved Guardian, the widow announced that those who wished might file by the coffin and pay their respects. They did, for over two hours and rarely in history, at least until that time, had there been such a demonstration of united love and grief. The morning had been sunny and fair, then softly a gentle shower started and sprinkled a few drops over the coffin as though nature herself were suddenly moved to tears.

When the last believers had filed by, Ruhiyyih Khanum approached the casket, kissed it, and knelt in prayer for a moment. She then had the green pall spread over it. On top of the pall she laid the blue and gold brocade from the innermost Shrine of Bahá'u'lláh, then arranged the still-fragrant jasmine flowers over the entire length. Finally the mortal remains of Shoghi Effendi were slowly lowered into the vault, amid walls covered with evergreen boughs and studded with flowers, to rest upon the rug brought from the Holy Tomb at Bahjí.

Prayers were then said in many languages, and floral offerings from the Holy Places were placed on the grave. Ruhiyyih Khanum wrote down all these details later in collaboration with English Hand of the Cause, John Ferraby. About this scene, she related:

> Over the tomb at his feet, like a shield of crimson and white, lay the fragrant sheath of blooms which had covered his casket, and heaped about was a rich carpet of exquisite flowers, symbols of the love, the suffering of so many hearts, and no doubt the silent bearers of vows to make the Spirit of the Guardian happy now, to fulfill his plans, carry on his work, be worthy at last of the love and inspired self-sacrificing leadership he gave them for thirty-six years of his life.

Many years later she told the friends how the monuments for the Guardian's grave came into being:

> ... After I had gone out and visited his grave the day after his funeral, as I drove away, it was very strange. . . . I saw before me in my mind's eye a column and a globe and an eagle and the steps underneath, the whole thing. And when

I went back to Haifa and the Hands of the Cause met in such trying circumstances . . . that first time, I showed them a little sketch and they were happy with it and they approved, and that was what we built over Shoghi Effendi's resting place.

Shoghi Effendi always wanted a column. Well, he got it, evidently. Every time we saw a beautiful column . . . he used to look at it and say, "I think these columns are so beautiful—*where* can I put a column on Mount Carmel?"

I said, "Shoghi Effendi, I don't think you can. You just can't stick a column up like that, you know. Where would you put it?" Well, he didn't have a column, but he wanted one.

He liked the Corinthian style very much and so I think that perhaps influenced my thought that we should have, perhaps, a column. . . . Then came the question of the eagle over Shoghi Effendi's grave. When he began to buy those eagles as ornaments for the gardens and put them up and we asked him why, he said it was a symbol of victory and that the Bahá'ís now all over the world were beginning to have their victories and the eagle was a symbol of victory and that was why he wanted to have an eagle in the gardens. So I thought—what greater place to put an eagle, the symbol of victory, than on top of Shoghi Effendi's column, on top of the globe of the world, with the continent of Africa which, at the end of his life, had already begun to show such promise, which had caused him so much joy, facing out, and we thought, what eagle should we put?

Then I remembered he had bought an eagle and had it in his room. . . . It was a Japanese eagle, very, very beautiful, and as you have seen from visiting his monument, it has one wing folded and one wing out. It's very hard to tell. Is the bird taking off or alighting? So, one night I brought it down in Shoghi Effendi's home—we got someone to hold it up in a corner and we looked at it and we felt that this was the perfect eagle for Shoghi Effendi's grave. . . .

Someone said that the wall around his grave looks so old. We tried to have something reminiscent of his beautiful gardens in Haifa here in his resting place. The red and the white and the ornaments, the iron gate, the gilding, something that was in *his* taste and along the lines of what he had created around the Holy Shrines. . . . If it seems old, it is because it came from a very famous estate. It *is* old and it is unusually beautiful. The Guardian loved beauty and I tried hard to surround his grave with the kind of beauty that seemed to be his taste....

The Hands of the Cause and the Auxiliary Board Members

IT WAS NOT yet nine days after the interment of Shoghi Effendi when the Hands of the Cause—then twenty-six of them—gathered at the World Center of their Faith, in their capacity as "Chief Stewards of the Embryonic World Commonwealth of Bahá'u'lláh" to consult together on the most tragic situation facing the Bahá'ís since the Ascension of 'Abdu'l-Bahá, and to do whatever was necessary and appropriate for the greatest welfare of the Bahá'í Faith.

The Hands of the Cause of God are an Institution of the Bahá'í Faith originally made to function by Bahá'u'lláh in His Own Lifetime, to aid in the development of the Faith. They form one of the most unique examples of a religious Institution dedicated to service and selflessness.

"The obligations of the Hands of the Cause of God," 'Abdu'l-Bahá had written, "are to diffuse the Divine Fragrances, to edify the souls of man, to promote learning, to improve the character of all men and to be, at all times and under all conditions, sanctified and detached from earthly things. They must manifest the fear of God by their conduct, their manners, their deeds and their words."

In 1953 the Guardian requested that the fifteen Hands residing outside the Holy Land appoint in each continent, from among the resident Bahá'ís there, Auxiliary Boards, the members of which would act as deputies, assistants, and advisors to the Hands. Each Auxiliary Board had a prescribed number of members for the time, not all of which were the same number, and all Boards were to report and be responsible to the Hands charged with their appointment. Later, when necessary, the numbers of Board members were increased in each continent.

In 1951 the Guardian had also formed the first International Bahá'í Council, as the forerunner of a Supreme Administrative Institution destined to eventually emerge for the Faith. This Council would forge a link with the newly emerged State of Israel. It would assist the Guardian in various of his responsibilities and would help to conduct any negotiations necessary with civil authorities on matters of personal status, plus any of its other functions gradually to evolve.

With the help of the Council, the international aspect of the Bahá'í Faith continued to progress. The exemption previously given concerning material gifts received for the Bahá'í Holy Places in Israel was extended by that government to cover all things received for the Western and Eastern Pilgrim Houses, plus the residence of the Head of the Faith. In addition the Israeli government was most understanding and cooperative about

Through efforts made by the believers at the World Center in Holy Places.

Haifa, year after year during the Guardian's lifetime, and since sent for the Shrine of the Báb and gifts intended for use in the then, the higher one goes in Israeli Government circles, the more obvious it is how very great is the courtesy shown to the Bahá'í Institutions, and the wider is the knowledge of the Bahá'í Faith possessed by government officials. Likewise, at high levels the Bahá'í International Headquarters personnel meet with ready reducing the heavy charges usually made in the port on material understanding, so that when assistance is needed by them, it is graciously given by representatives of Israel.

On November 19, 1957, nine Hands of the Cause from the Holy Land, Africa, Asia, Europe, and the United States, representing beloved Guardian's rooms in Haifa and scrutinized his papers. senting the several continents of the East and West, among them the Guardian's widow, broke the seals placed upon the appointed during Shoghi Effendi's lifetime, assembled in the These same Hands, rejoining the remaining Hands who had been

Mansion of Bahá'u'lláh at Bahjí, and announced that Shoghi Effendi had left no Will and Testament.

The Guardian as an individual left no property. His home, whatever he had collected in all those years of service, belonged to the Faith.

In addition, it was likewise certified that he had left no heir. He and Ruhiyyih Khanum had no children. There were no Bahá'í relatives spiritually or morally able to fit the requirements laid down by 'Abdu'l-Bahá for a Successor to the Guardian, to be the next Sign of God on Earth.

These facts placed a heavy burden, indeed, on the Hands. But they realized that the Dispensation of Bahá'u'lláh which had so quickened the powers and resources of faith within mankind was certainly not going to stop there, but would continue to help achieve the unity and progression required for the believers. In this new light of understanding, the group of Hands was able to perceive in detail the very many blessings which Shoghi Effendi had created and left as his true legacy to the loyal body of believers:

Had not the World Center, with its sacred Shrines and Institutions, been firmly established? Had not the Message been established by that time in 254 countries and dependencies, and the necessary National and Regional Assemblies been implanted in so many great areas of all continents? And had not the Guardian left the believers not only his incomparable translations of the Bahá'í Sacred Literature, but also his own masterworks of interpretation which discloses to them the unshatterable edifice of an evolving Bahá'í Order and world community?

Had not the Guardian, building upon the enduring foundation of the Master's Tablets of the Divine Plan, created the World Crusade to guide their Bahá'í work until 1963?

And finally, had not the Guardian, with his mysterious insight into the present and future needs of the Bahá'í community, called into being the company of Hands with their Auxiliary Boards and, in his final communication to the Bahá'ís, had he not designated the Hands as "Chief Stewards of the Embryonic World Commonwealth of Bahá'u'lláh"?

In their capacity the Hands decided to constitute a body of nine of their members to serve at the Bahá'í World Center in order to deal energetically with the protection and promotion of the Faith.

This same body of nine was to maintain correspondence with Hands working in the several continents, with National Assemblies, and would assist such National Assemblies on matters involving administrative questions. And, this body's most awesome and inspiring decision was to supervise the International Bahá'í Council in arranging the election and formation of the Universal House of Justice, the goal toward which the Guardian had obviously been working.

Despite or because of their grief for the loss of the Guardian, the Hands worked harder than ever. Many of them traveled to Regional International Conferences that Shoghi Effendi had already arranged, encouraging the national and local administrative groups in their own efforts, and keeping the believers constantly apprised of new victories, new goals, and new incentives.

The voice of Shoghi Effendi was heard over and over again through talks and cables and letters from the Hands. All around the Bahá'í world he remained a living figure, an inspiration to constant effort and achievement, just as when he was alive. His place was assured—not the Place occupied by the Báb, Bahá'u'lláh and 'Abdu'l-Bahá, but his own place as Guardian, the reverence for someone who had truly been divinely guided and in so being had guided them more swiftly, more surely, to their destiny of world evolvement than anyone had ever believed possible.

The Universal House of Justice — The Bahá'í Supreme Body

ALTHOUGH EVERY Bahá'í is familiar with the spiritual authority conferred upon the Universal House of Justice by Bahá'u'lláh and 'Abdu'l-Bahá, for the uninitiate it is necessary to quote some of the passages from 'Abdu'l-Bahá's Will and Testament, which set forth the divine promises and injunctions relating to the establishment of this august Institution:

> . . . concerning the House of Justice which God hath ordained as the source of all good and freed from all error, it must be elected by universal suffrage, that is, by the believers. Its members must be manifestations of the fear of God and daysprings of knowledge and understanding, must be steadfast in God's faith and the well-wishers of all mankind. By this House is meant the Universal House of Justice, that is, in all countries a secondary House of Justice [National Spiritual Assembly is the name by which they are still called at this time] must be instituted, and these secondary Houses of Justice must elect the members of the Universal one. Unto this body all things must be referred. It enacteth all ordinances and regulations that are not to be found in the explicit Holy Text.

> The sacred and youthful branch, the guardian of the Cause of God as well as the Universal House of Justice, to be universally elected and established, are both under the care and protection of the Abha Beauty [Bahá'u'lláh], under the shelter and unerring guidance of His Holiness, the Exalted One (may my life be offered up for them both). Whatsoever they decide is of God. Whoso obeyeth him not, neither obeyeth them, hath not obeyed God; whoso rebelleth against him and against them hath rebelled against God; whoso opposeth him hath opposed God; whoso contendeth with them hath contended with God. . . .

> This is the foundation of the belief of the people of Bahá. . . ."His Holiness, the Exalted One [the Báb], is the manifestation of the Unity and Oneness of God and the forerunner of the Ancient Beauty. His Holiness the Abha Beauty . . . is the Supreme Manifestation of God and the Daysprings of His Most Divine Essence. All others are servants unto Him and do His bidding." Unto the Most Holy Book every one must turn and all that is not expressly recorded therein must be referred to the Universal House of Justice. That which this body, whether unanimously or by a majority doth carry, that

is verily the Truth and the Purpose of God Himself. Whoso doth deviate therefrom is verily of them that love discord, hath shown forth malice and turned away from the Lord of the Covenant.

All must seek guidance and turn unto the Center of the Cause and the House of Justice. And he that turneth unto whatsoever else is indeed in grievous error.

In many of his writings during his ministry, the Guardian explained the functions of the House of Justice and described the bounties which would descend upon the world following its establishment. He made it clear that Bahá'u'lláh's promise that "God will verily inspire them with whatsoever He willeth" referred to the Institution of the House of Justice acting as the consultative body having the "exclusive right and prerogative . . . to pronounce upon and deliver the final judgment on such laws and ordinances as Bahá'u'lláh had not expressly revealed."

In a cabled message sent early in 1951 commenting on the participation of four National Spiritual Assemblies in the newly opened African teaching campaign which was to bring such joy to his heart, Shoghi Effendi gave an indication of the future role of the Universal House of Justice in linking the various Baha'í National Assemblies in world-wide undertakings:

FERVENTLY PRAYING PARTICIPATION BRITISH, AMERICAN, PERSIAN, EGYPTIAN NATIONAL ASSEMBLIES UNIQUE, EPOCH-MAKING ENTERPRISE AFRICAN CONTINENT MAY PROVE PRE-LUDE CONVOCATION FIRST AFRICAN TEACHING CONFERENCE LEADING EVENTUALLY INITIATION UNDERTAKINGS INVOLVING COLLABORATION ALL NATIONAL ASSEMBLIES OF BAHA'I WORLD THEREBY PAVING WAY ULTIMATE ORGANIC UNION THESE ASSEMBLIES THROUGH FORMATION INTERNATIONAL HOUSE OF JUSTICE DESTINED LAUNCH ENTERPRISES EMBRACING WHOLE BAHA'I WORLD.

However, since the friends knew that the Guardian's efforts were toward the eventual election of a Universal House of Justice, the situation of his having passed on without appointing a Successor presented an obscure question not covered by the explicit Bahá'í Holy Text.

The Hands announced that it would have to be referred to the Universal House of Justice. Before the formation of this House of Justice, there had been *no knowledge at all that there would be no Second Guardian.* Therefore, an election at the end of the Ten-Year Crusade was obviously necessary and accordingly announced by the Hands.

From the very outset of their custodianship of the Cause of God, the Hands realized that since there was no certainty of divine guidance for them such as was incontrovertibly assured to the Guardian and the Universal House of Justice, the one safe course was to follow with undeviating firmness the instructions and policies of Shoghi Effendi. The entire history of religion shows no comparable record of such strict self-discipline, such absolute loyalty, and such complete self-abnegation by the leaders of a religion who had found themselves suddenly deprived of their divinely inspired guide.

The Guardian had given the Bahá'í world explicit and detailed plans covering the period until Riḍván (April) 1963, the end of the Ten-Year Crusade. From that point, unless the Faith were to be endangered, further divine guidance was absolutely necessary, still another pressing reason to call the election of the Universal House of Justice. The rightness of the time was further confirmed by references found in letters by Shoghi Effendi to the fact that the Ten-Year Crusade, his last, would be followed by other plans under the direction of the Universal House of Justice.

Having been in charge of the Cause of God for six years the Hands, with absolute faith and reliance in the Bahá'í Holy Writings, called upon the believers of the Faith, through their National Assembly delegates, to elect the Universal House of Justice, and even went so far as to ask that the Hands themselves not be voted for.

During the twelve days of Riḍván 1963 the elected representatives of the fifty-six national and regional communities of the Bahá'í World were called to elect the members of the Universal House of Justice. This was done at Haifa, and was followed by a series of celebrations at the London World Congress of Bahá'ís at Albert Hall, attended by nearly seven thousand believers from all over the world. It was climaxed by a visit to Shoghi Effendi's last earthly resting place.

All of this coincided with the termination of the late Guardian's Ten-Year World Crusade, a stage in itself in the unfoldment of the Divine Plan of 'Abdu'l-Bahá, and made fact His statement that the establishment of the Universal House of Justice would be "that last unit crowning the structure of the embryonic World Order of Bahá'u'lláh." The believers also feel that, as Shoghi Effendi predicted, the election of this glorious Institution "will be regarded by posterity as the last refuge of a tottering civilization."

Finally the celebrants of all races, colors, and backgrounds went back to their homes and the new nine-member International Administrative Body of the far-flung Bahá'í world settled down to work in Haifa, together with the Hands in residence there. The International Council's work was finished. Henceforth the Bahá'ís must turn to their Universal House of Justice as their divinely inspired, divinely guided body. None of its nine members, by mutual decision, would be singled out for individual attention or praise, if possible. They would refuse to look back at any of the circumstances or personal problems that had led to them and, in most instances, their families, taking up residence in Haifa to help mold this embryonic institution of the Universal House of Justice.

Sufficient to say that each member of the Universal House of Justice *has* given up his own way of life to the service of his Faith. The nine members come from various countries and backgrounds, but they are united as one soul, one heart, one purpose representing the unification of the believers, and the oneness of mankind, according to the Laws and Teachings of the Bahá'í Faith.

Uniquely, the House of Justice has appointed no officers. It has no set term of office, either, except what the House may decide for itself. The first body decided on its term as five years, and the next election for 1968. They revolve the chairmanship and carry out their work under department headings and subdepartmental procedures which have been decided upon at meetings of the body. Each member of the House also serves in more than one department and all reports from National Assemblies are read by the members of this international body.

The Universal House of Justice is now the center of the Bahá'í Faith, its supreme body, and is considered by the believers to be their "infallible source of *divine* guidance." Today the work is many times greater than it was during the Guardian's lifetime, and the task of the Hands, the Auxiliary Board members, the various Assemblies, the entire International Administration and the body of believers is correspondingly increased.

It is therefore amazing to those unacquainted with Bahá'í determination to note how very quickly and thoroughly the Universal House of Justice has coped with its structure. The primary responsibilities of the Hands is now teaching and protection of the Faith and that body, while separated from the direct working of the Administrative Order, acts as consultants to the House maintaining a very close working relationship with it.

The Hands of the Cause throughout the world send in their reports, requests, or suggestions to the Hands residing in Haifa who, in turn, pass these and their own suggestions to the Universal House of Justice. The House, then, in consultation with the Hands, decides the assignment of Hands to continents, since the ultimate authority for all matters in the Bahá'ís Faith is now vested in this supreme body.

Since the function of the House is administration, not interpretation, its members are still very cautious about using the authority implicit in Shoghi Effendi's written statement that "the Universal House of Justice has the exclusive right and prerogative

. . . to pronounce and deliver the final judgment on such laws and ordinances as Bahá'u'lláh has not expressly revealed."

For legislation, their process is very solemn and thorough. Every available Bahá'í text is researched for the problem at hand, every possible avenue is gleaned for knowledge, illumination, and guidance. The Hands in Haifa are called in to contribute whatever they may know from Bahá'í research and texts for that particular instance. Everything in these texts is studied very carefully by the House. If there still is something that is not absolutely clear to it, it keeps searching and researching before finally making a decision that stems from most careful consultation of all House members in formal session.

The principle of consultation is basic in every aspect of Bahá'í life, work, and function. Therefore, it is equally a guiding principle in the work of the international administration and is never a hurried affair, and is always preceded with special prayers for divine guidance.

And not the least part of the Universal House of Justice's work is to see that every plan, every hope, every accomplishment of the Guardian is fulfilled just as he desired, so that in years to come, just as now, this will be the first great religion that could not be shattered from within, because it is the *only* religion, the Bahá'ís feel, to stick to the precepts that have been laid down by its Planners.

The Archives Building and Holy Relics of the Faith in Haifa

NO BOOK about the Bahá'í Faith can pretend to be complete without mention of the thorough manner in which Shoghi Effendi, its first Guardian, helped to collate, collect, and bring to permanent custody of the Bahá'ís those artifacts that bring their history alive.

As has been noted elsewhere in these pages, the Guardian used to share with Ruhiyyih Khanum, his wife, everything he did during the day, showing her diagrams and plans for projects that were being developed in the Holy Places of their Faith. When he was telling her the minutest details of why he had bought all the ornamental Japanese and Chinese furniture and objets d'art for the Archives, and other ideas pertaining to the building, she subconsciously absorbed everything but didn't stop to consider *why* all this was being given to her. For instance, he had told her where he wanted to put each piece of furniture, that the truly glorious Chinese rug should be placed exactly in the center of the long room on the main floor, which table would be placed on the rug, and which ornament should go on the object.

Therefore, the Archives Building is a blending of the personalities of both Shoghi Effendi and Ruhiyyih Khanum, since he selected everything and she supervised their placement after his death. It had taken three years to build the Archives structure, but the interior decoration was not finished before his final visit to London where he selected many more of its furnishings.

When Ruhiyyih Khanum undertook to finish the interior project, she realized how very much, indeed, the Guardian had detailed to her. The original Archives Building had been the three rooms nearest to the mountain, in the Báb's Shrine. Much of the old furniture was brought from there and used in the new building.

The Archives is the first building of a series of international buildings that will eventually be built around the Arc that is a semicircle inside the gardens. These are planned to include the Universal House of Justice Building and the International Library, among other edifices.

When you walk into the Archives Building—which is opened only for visits from Bahá'í pilgrims—you find yourself in a long, oblong room, at the end of which is a large, wide window of stained glass in red, yellow, and blue squares that catch your breath with their beauty. The three cabinets at the end of the floor have pictures of Bahá'u'lláh done by an Armenian artist.

One shows Bahá'u'lláh in a gesture of benediction that is not Islámic, but Christian, done from an artistic conception that is the painter's own spiritual reflection of Bahá'u'lláh. The Bahá'ís have been told that the colors on these paintings are quite true to life, particularly the mouth, as Bahá'u'lláh is said to have had beautiful, very red lips.

The cabinet to the left of this long room shows the only photograph of Bahá'u'lláh, taken in Adrianople, which demonstrates how much He had changed in that seven- or eight-year period because of His great suffering.

The cabinet to the right has the only miniature portrait of the Báb in existence. It was painted during one of the periods when He was being transported from another prison to Tabríz, at the time of an incident with a wild horse. His tormentors hoped to humiliate Him, but the horse proved gentle until the Báb had dismounted, and instead the crowds had flocked to see Him for three days. Among these people was this artist. Every time the Báb saw him, even though they had never before met and had never spoken, He would fix His attire and resume the same position, as though conscious of truly posing for His portrait.

The artist drew many pencil sketches and later completed the actual painting. He also became a Bábí and sent the finished portrait to Bahá'u'lláh. An uncle of the Báb who was with Bahá'u'lláh said it was a true portrait of his Nephew. Then it was returned to the artist by Bahá'u'lláh Who asked that he put in as much color as he could remember. A copy of this portrait is in the American Bahá'í Temple at Wilmette, Illinois, along with a copy of the portrait of Bahá'u'lláh in the attitude of benediction.

There can also be seen here some beautiful cabinets which contain portrait miniatures of 'Abdu'l-Bahá and other photographs and paintings of Him.

The portraits were originally kept in the room of the Greatest Holy Leaf, Bahá'u'lláh's daughter, together with many other precious relics now safeguarded in the Archives. The frames for these portraits are made of rare silver and gold Chinese filigree sent from China for this particular purpose.

The Archives also contain the letters the Báb sent to His eighteen "Letters of the Living." The original samples of Bahá'u'-lláh's Tablets are on view and a Persian artist who was invited to Haifa by the Guardian took many months to finish illuminating these Tablets in the traditional Persian manner.

The Báb's letters to His eighteen original disciples tell them to serve, to have faith, and to go out and teach the Message He had brought for mankind. He addresses them by the number in which each disciple appeared. At the time these letters were written, the Báb also wrote one to Bahá'u'lláh, addressing the Founder of the Bahá'í Dispensation as "He Whom God Shall Make Manifest."

A piece of the Báb's shirt, with blood on it from His martyrdom, is on display. There are exhibited pieces of dried leaves from His House in Shíráz, some cuttings from His nails, and a wood shaving from His coffin. This shaving was secured when 'Abdu'l-Bahá, at last able to place the rescued Remains of the Báb in the marble sarcophagus at Haifa, in the Shrine, discovered that the original coffin in which He had been placed was slightly larger than the receptacle intended for it. It had to be shaved down to the exact measurements.

One letter by the Báb addresses His beloved wife as "All the Sweetness of My Soul," and was written to her from one of His places of imprisonment.

Bahá'u'lláh had several seals for use during His ministry and some are shown. Many letters on each wall of the Archives building are those addressed by 'Abdu'l-Bahá to the Greatest Holy Leaf, when she represented Him during His travels abroad. Some included various instructions for the members of the Household, since she was its Head during His absences. Each one was written in very affectionate terms, showing the great bond of love between them.

One says in part: "I wish you were here to see with your own eyes how the Religion of our Father is spreading in the West."

In a Tablet He wrote, "I testify that you have suffered more than anyone in this Family, and I assure you that in the Worlds to come you and I both will forget everything else because we shall be close to our Father. . . ."

One time 'Abdu'l-Bahá was in Beirut, and the letter is in the Archives by Bahá'u'lláh to Him: "Blessed is the land where Thy foot has stopped."

These were considered so precious by the Guardian that he would not have them changed one iota, even for decoration, and they are framed as they were when found.

When 'Abdu'l-Bahá went to America, He longed to take Shoghi Effendi with Him, but for many reasons could not do so. Many of His letters written to Haifa at that time are filled with the most beautiful phrases of love for His very special grandson.

A number of the objets d'art in this Archives Building are not Bahá'í items, but were purchased only for the sake of their beauty, because the Guardian had announced that he would not sacrifice beauty for utility. Neither would he ever pay too much for any of them, no matter how beautiful or special or desirable it might appear. If there was a choice between later antiquity in one item over another, he would select the more beautiful, albeit the less antique one. Many of them were donated by the Bahá'ís.

Ruhiyyih Khanum told many of the friends how the diverse arts of the Far East and Europe could blend well together. The Chinese and Japanese cabinets are of teak and gold lacquer; other cabinets on the main floor have red and green stenciled doors, and all were chosen by Shoghi Effendi.

The Guardian had bought eight panels in London. When Ruhiyyih Khanum was decorating the Archives Building, she knew he had meant them for use there, but was unable to think of where to put them. After days of effort, she decided to use them as door-to-wall cabinets, so that the Tablets of Bahá'u'lláh could be displayed inside them.

There are many fragile and delicate ornaments which are intended only for decoration and beauty. Four delicately made center cabinets are filled with relics of Bahá'u'lláh. Locks of His hair are there, saved only through the wisdom and vision of the Greatest Holy Leaf. Every time she was in His Presence, she would collect His hair, strand by strand from His comb. She never threw the strands away, but arranged them in a frame in the form of locks with curled ends, just as He used to wear them.

In some precious boxes is dried blood of Bahá'u'lláh, from the custom of spring blood-letting, which was supposedly good for the health. Again, the Greatest Holy Leaf collected this blood and dried it, and it looks like dark brown specks in the receptacles.

One year when the Guardian and his wife were away, she begged permission to order a special box to contain some of the blood of Bahá'u'lláh. She designed a gold spray set with semiprecious stones and this was mounted on a beautiful ivory box with the jeweled decoration on its lid.

There are prayer beads used by Bahá'u'lláh, a purse used by Him, a Turkish coin, a snuff box, and Bahá'u'lláh's cap (which was called a táj and is of a different height and type than what was known as a fez).

The Guardian asked the believers all over Persia to send in their own precious relics of Bahá'u'lláh to the Archives, and there are many different things, including prayer beads and boxes that He had given out in abundance.

Bahá'u'lláh's reed pen—the same kind many Persians still use today— is on exhibit, along with the knives used to sharpen it. Even His pen box with the small silver receptacle for ink which he would mix with water. There are broken cords from prayer beads He used, and several impressions from His seals which are put together in a photostated montage. There is even a sliver of the soap used on His Body after His death, before He was buried.

It took Ruhíyyih Khánum over two years to finish placing everything just the way she thought the Guardian would want them in these Archives. Many of the shelves are decorated with antique pieces of brocade that she cut out into lovely doilies. She used the precious materials she had collected for years for lining the cabinets and shelves, to beautify the Archives as she thought the Guardian would have liked them to be.

One shirt exhibited was made by hand by a Bahá'í who received Bahá'u'lláh's permission to do this. On the shirt is the letter of thanks sent to the Bahá'í by Bahá'u'lláh, which her family later sent to the Guardian.

There are cotton caps exhibited which were worn under the táj to collect perspiration and to help keep the táj unstained.

Also on exhibit is the alms bowl He carried during the two years He lived in the mountains as a dervish. His slippers and puttees are shown, and the sponge was preserved with which His body was washed for burial.

From His period in Baghdád one can see the very worn shirts. There was a time when Bahá'u'lláh had only one shirt and had to wait for it to be washed and dried before He could wear it again. Those were the days of far greater suffering and hardship, possibly, than were most of His other days. There are also to be seen a nightcap, a small locket with some cuttings from His nails, a tea strainer, a few of the spoons He used, some sugar resembling rock candy which had been used as a kind of medicine, and many of His cloaks.

Every time soap was used by Bahá'u'lláh the last tiny sliver was saved. There are shown the bowls He used for pouring water over Himself during His personal ablutions. The clothes from His later life give the believers the feeling that perhaps during His last few years He had a few more items of wearing apparel. There were no ties worn in those days. Everything appears to have been collarless, and the shirts were very long.

The photographs shown of Bahá'u'lláh's youngest son, the

Purest Branch, with 'Abdu'l-Bahá, were taken at the same time as the picture of Bahá'u'lláh in Adrianople.

Many of the articles in the Archives add up to a unique documentary of the personal habits of each of these glorious martyrs to the New Faith. To see them is to have each believer's heart break a little in wonder and appreciation of the cost to Them for bringing God's lastest Message to mankind. Words can only fail to capture the special spiritual meaning of each item, and only a little of the sacred history intended to be read in their display can be gathered at one viewing.

'Abdu'l-Bahá often gave His prayer beads to those who visited Him. He frequently wore high boots, having suffered from severe frostbite at the age of eight when those with Bahá'u'lláh traversed the mountains after leaving Ṭihrán. In the summer He wore boots that were light in weight and usually white in color. He was always very fond of binoculars and when He returned from His visit to the West, He brought a number of them back as gifts. Shoghi Effendi had inherited this same fondness for binoculars.

'Abdu'l-Bahá seldom owned two coats at the same time, since He often gave these away also. In the summer His coat was white. The believers visiting Him would bring heavy winter coats for Him to wear in cold weather. He would put one on, go for a walk, and then return minus the coat. He had given it away to someone who needed it more than He did. He already had another one and felt that one would suffice Him.

In one instance an Arab asked for something "from Effendi." 'Abdu'l-Bahá gave him a beautiful heavy wool coat. The man asked surlily, "Is it cotton or wool?" The Master showed him that it was pure wool, then pointed to His own garment and remarked, " 'Abdu'l-Bahá wears cotton, but for His guests only the best—wool!"

There are some silver spoons displayed in the Archives which have 'Abdu'l-Bahá's name engraved on them. They were sent by friends He met in His foreign travels during His last years, particularly those in America. In New York City He had been given an engraved cup made of solid silver, the size of a loving cup. It had been presented at a special Bahá'í Feast where 'Abdu'l-Bahá drank water from it, then passed it around to all present so they could share its contents also. It stands proudly in its place in an Archives cabinet.

There is a gold pen box given to Him which had never been used. Like His Father, He preferred to use the cheap pen box of little value at the time, which is also on exhibit.

'Abdu'l-Bahá used some herbs as medicine, and displayed is His own prescription for these, in His own handwriting. There are also some seals, some rose water, even His medical thermometer, preserved for history, and some framed samples of His hair from two different stages of His life, which had been preserved as precious relics by family members.

Displayed predominantly on one wall is the huge enlargement of a photograph taken of 'Abdu'l-Bahá when in Philadelphia.

The Mother of 'Abdu'l-Bahá was know as Buyuk Khanum, "Great Lady" in Turkish. There is preserved a lovely, personal letter from her to Him, written as any mother would write to her son. The Bahá'í guide who takes Bahá'í pilgrims through the Archives Building is usually the wife of one of the Hands or House of Justice Members living in Haifa and translates this lettter of Buyuk Khanum as a message of love for her unique Son. She is said to have had a fabulous trousseau which forty mules carried to the House of Bahá'u'lláh when they were married. She was able to rescue only a few of her precious things when They were imprisoned, selling many of them gradually during their ten years in Baghdád, for money to live on. One thing she did not sell is an old-fashioned embroidered box which she took into exile. There it stands in the Archives.

There are many trophies of the Greatest Holy Leaf, 'Abdu'l-Bahá's sister, who was Shoghi Effendi's Great-Aunt. During the time the Guardian was away after 'Abdu'l-Bahá's death, she wrote a number of letters to the Persian friends, encouraging them, telling them to arise and gather around Shoghi Effendi, describing how blessed they all were to have this radiant soul to guide them, and so forth.

The Greatest Holy Leaf's clothing and many personal mementoes are shown to the believers and explained. She was a very immaculate person who loved children. Always she carried candy in her purse for them, and would give them sweets or coins. She had a very special station in the Family as the Grand Lady or Senior Lady. She lived to her eighties, but had to be in bed most of the time during her last years, as she was very frail. She was very beloved and very precious to those fortunate enough to have been near her even for a short time.

There is a picture of the day when 'Abdu'l-Bahá was knighted in Haifa by General Allenby of the British occupancy in the name of the King of England. In the picture, 'Abdu'l-Bahá is sitting a bit in front of the actual reviewing stand, looking as though He is trying to be patient but wishing the whole unnecessary nuisance were over. General Allenby had sent a special carriage to bring 'Abdu'l-Bahá to the place of honor, but when it arrived He couldn't be found. Everyone was concerned and then to their amazement He showed up—on foot. He didn't want anyone to think it was such a "big" thing, His being knighted, or such a special occasion. It ended with General Allenby realizing that actually it was *his* government being honored, not 'Abdu'l-Bahá.

The late Winston Churchill signed the knighthood document, but 'Abdu'l-Bahá never used the title. He said that He only accepted the knighthood as a sign of righteous government but He never accepted it for Himself, personally.

Only a few things are shown as of now that belonged to the Guardian, but they too emphasize the modesty in his clothing and personal tastes. He often wore the same overcoat from the time of his marriage to the time of his passing, twenty years later.

One of the things displayed was a volume of Gibbon's *Decline*

and Fall of the Roman Empire, which he had with him in London
when he died. It was a favorite book of the Guardian.

If ever there was needed true proof of the fact that Shoghi
Effendi, Guardian of the Bahá'í Faith, had lived only to preserve
the Cause of God, the effort that he made to enshrine all that
was mortally possible to preserve of its history is more than proof
enough. He never planned for anything of his own to be a
part of it.

The records of items in the Archives are locked away
with their history, annotating how they were originally secured
by the individuals who had sent them in, or by their ancestors.

Each item has been certified to be genuine or the Guardian
would not have approved its being shown. The members of the
Universal House of Justice and the Hands living in Haifa will
continue to follow this same method of certification for any
other Bahá'í historical contributions offered for inclusion in this
or future Archives.

America's Destiny
in the Baha'i World

America and the New Faith

FROM THE TIME 'Abdu'l-Bahá visited the continent of North America, the believers there felt that they were destined to play a special part in the development of the new Faith, not only in their own country, but in any part of the universe where they were called upon to serve.

Until April 1948 the American and Canadian Bahá'ís were part of one National Administrative Order and worked as one, also. Then the Guardian felt that the Canadians had grown spiritually and in Bahá'í numbers sufficiently to have their own administrative body, and from that time on the Bahá'ís in the United States and in Canada each had separate goals with a unified aim—to promote the Faith and to help it grow wherever the Guardian requested.

Both the Canadian and American believers had always done their utmost to fulfill every need placed before them in the Name of Bahá'u'lláh. They have always evidenced a spontaneous loyalty to the wishes of 'Abdu'l-Bahá, as expressed in His Last Will and Testament and they have repeatedly given spiritual and material comfort to the needy and harassed believers in less fortunate areas. They have even resisted and overcome the shameless attacks of vicious enemies of the Faith who tried to cut down its rapid growth.

In America at least one member of the press did not hesitate to castigate this new religion, without trying to base his remarks upon proven fact. On November 3, 1948, while the members of the new, separate National Spiritual Assembly of the Bahá'ís of the United States were preparing for their meeting that week, this syndicated newspaperman's column included the statement:

"I do, however, venture a fearless rejection of babism as a hellish doctrine . . . a Persian delusion . . . known as Bahá'í."

Another religious group might have sued or sought revenge through friendlier members of the daily press, but this is not the Bahá'í way. Following their principle of nonviolence, they used a softer, more effective method, one that might possibly have resembled "the other cheek" to those less astute about such "soft sell," even in religious matters. The Bahá'ís paid for space in *Editor & Publisher* and one other journalistic trade publication of the time to explain to all the members of the press reading those publications about the persecutions suffered by the Faith in Persia, Turkey, Nazi Germany, and Soviet Russia. This "ad" told about the spread of the teachings at that time to ninety-one countries, and gave the basic principles of the Faith. Emphasis was placed upon pointing out the blasphemous nature of the offending journalist's inaccuracies, and a pamphlet was offered for any journalist desiring it that summarized the history and teachings of the Bahá'ís.

This episode is significant because it demonstrates the Bahá'í belief in the miraculous power of their Revelation to press forward by making use of detractors as well as friends to spread the Message. In writing about this to the believers, their National Assembly was most reassuring:

Perhaps some of the new believers, startled by such an unexpected attack in a paper read by their friends and neighbors, might be reminded of the Master's assurance expressed during His visit to America in 1912, that when the Faith shall be bitterly assailed and denounced from all sides, its numbers will grow with amazing rapidity. Nothing from outside can harm the Faith of Bahá'u'lláh. On the contrary, attempts to harm it will redound to its benefit and prove a blessing in disguise.

Further stimulation of the belief that America's destiny was to be a special one has come from many of Shoghi Effendi's writings to the American believers. In 1938 he stated:

> ... The distance that the American nation has traveled ... the changes that have unexpectedly overtaken it in recent years ... are to every Bahá'í observer ... most significant. ...
>
> Nothing, however, can alter eventually that course ordained for it by the unerring pen of 'Abdu'l-Bahá. ...

In his long communiqué outlining the requirements for North American believers detailed in 'Abdu'l-Bahá's Divine Plan, Shoghi Effendi reminded them that 'Abdu'l-Bahá had written that before long the North American believers (which at that time included reference to the Canadians, of course) would "witness how brilliantly every one of you, even as a shining star, will radiate in the firmament of your country the light of divine guidance, and will bestow upon its people the glory of an ever-lasting life. . . ."

The Guardian continued by describing the parallel between the American Bahá'í community and the American Republic:

> Might not still a closer parallel be drawn between the community singled out for the execution of this world-embracing Plan, in its relation to its sister communities, and the nation of which it forms a part, in its relation to its sister nations? On the one hand is a community which ever since its birth has been nursed in the lap of 'Abdu'l-Bahá and been lovingly trained by Him through the revelation of unnumbered Tablets, through the dispatch of special and successive Messengers, and through His own prolonged visit to the North American continent in the evening of His life. It was to the members of this community, the spiritual descendants of the dawn-breakers of the Heroic Age of our Faith, that He, whilst sojourning in the City of the Covenant, chose to reveal the implications of that Covenant. It was in the vicinity of this community's earliest established center that He laid, with His own hands, the cornerstone of the first Mashriqu'l-Adhkár of

the Western world. It was to the members of this community that He subsequently addressed His Tablets of the Divine Plan, investing it with a spiritual primacy and singling it out for a glorious mission among its sister communities. It was this community which won the immortal honor of being the first to introduce the Faith in the British Isles, in France, and in Germany, and which sent forth its consecrated pioneers and teachers to China, Japan, and India, to Australia and New Zealand, to the Balkan Peninsula, to South Africa, to Latin America, to the Baltic States, to Scandinavia and the islands of the Pacific, hoisting thereby its banner in the vast majority of the countries won over to its cause, in both the East and the West, prior to 'Abdu'l-Bahá's passing.

It was this community, the cradle and stronghold of the Administrative Order of the Faith of Bahá'u'lláh, which, on the morrow of 'Abdu'l-Bahá's ascension, was the first among all other Bahá'í communities in East and West to arise and champion the cause of that Order, to fix its pattern, to erect its fabric, to initiate its endowments, to establish and consolidate its subsidiary institutions, and to vindicate its aims and purposes. . . .

On the other hand is a nation that has achieved undisputed ascendancy in the entire Western Hemisphere, whose rulers have been uniquely honored by being collectively addressed by the Author of the Bahá'í Revelation . . . ; which has been acclaimed by 'Abdu'l-Bahá as the "home of the righteous and the gathering-place of the free," where the "splendors of His light shall be revealed, where the mysteries of His Faith shall be unveiled" and belonging to a continent which, as recorded by that same pen, "giveth signs and evidences of very great advancement," whose "future is even more promising," whose "influence and illumination are far-reaching," and which "will lead all nations spiritually." . . . It is in connection with its people that He has affirmed that they are "indeed worthy of being the first to build the Tabernacle of the Great Peace and proclaim the oneness of mankind."

Finally, in a letter dated September 21, 1957, just before His death, the beloved Guardian of the Bahá'ís wrote to them:

[Americans] cannot be the chosen people of God—the ones who have received the bounty of accepting Him in His Day, the recipients of the Master's Divine Plan—and do nothing about it. The obligation to teach is the obligation of every Bahá'í, and particularly the obligations of the American Bahá'ís toward humanity are great and inescapable. . . .

. . . The Bahá'ís are the leaven of God, which must leaven the lump of their nation. . . .

The National Spiritual Assembly of the United States

CONSIDERING THE description of the functions of the local Spiritual Assembly, which has nine members, one can realize that the National Assembly is an extension of this branch, with many of its duties performed in the same attitude of selflessness, Bahá'í love, and prayerful consideration, but with many more duties and many more concerns of its own.

There are sixty-nine national administrative bodies in the Faith, representing every country of the world. Each such national body is on call twenty-four hours a day, each has nine members who must be prepared to help resolve whatever situation may suddenly arise.

Nothing is too small or too large to be handled by these National Spiritual Assemblies, whether it is done by telephonic consultation or at the regular meetings,

The National Spiritual Assembly of the Bahá'ís of the United States, like all national Bahá'í bodies, is concerned with the spiritual and practical matters affecting the proctection and propagation of the Faith in America. Like any large organization, there is a great deal of work that cannot be individually taken care of by only the Assembly members, but must be funneled through committees or individuals selected by that body. Later committee or individual reports on such funneled matters are given to the national body to keep it apprised of the current status of the work.

Members of the National Assembly attend its monthly meetings in Wilmette, Illinois, the national headquarters, or, as occasionally does happen, at one of the American Bahá'í summer schools or any other special area considered necessary for that purpose at some given time. Each member of the national body can be appointed, if necessary, to represent it in giving talks, making appearances at Bahá'í functions or state conventions, or as a member of a committee, but when not representing the Assembly specifically his role is the same in Bahá'í affairs of his own community or any other Bahá'í commuAuity as that of any other individual Bahá'í in good standing.

More than one may realize, members of elected Bahá'í assemblies—national or local—attempt to follow the conditions laid down by 'Abdu'l-Bahá on how to live the Bahá'í life. They are usually modest, unassuming individuals who have been elected by their Bahá'í brothers and sisters because their devotion, their effectiveness, and their abilities have been brought to the attention of the electorate in some special way, but never through any kind of electioneering. Such individuals try not to stand out in the Bahá'í work they accomplish, but since each elected member seems automatically to combine the necessary qualities of enthusiasm, energy, devotion to the Faith, spiritual capacity, and dedication to teaching the Faith in some way, it can be understood why their endeavors are so soon noticed and the qualities recognized by the other believers in elections.

The American national headquarters of the Faith are remarkable to see. These include magnificent gardens, various office buildings, including their own modern Publishing Trust for the Bahá'í books, various residences nearby, and other accommodations. Because of the vast office duties of the national secretariat, the present arrangement permits an elected assistant who is a member of the Assembly and also lives in Wilmette near the headquarters. Naturally, the Office of Secretary is the most burdensome and therefore demands not only his full time but that of his assistant.

The national offices at Wilmette remain open at least six days a week, and often for seven days. Apart from the elected officers of the secretariat, the office personnel are Bahá'ís who have been especially recruited because of their special skills and qualifications for these tasks and often insist on working six and seven days a week without being asked when they know a specific Teaching Campaign, Conference, or Convention is coming up which requires additional cooperation. In fact, many of the Bahá'í office workers and committee members, paid or volunteer, vie for the privilege of helping out at Wilmette around the clock during such "rush" and "peak" sessions.

Considering the current wide aspect and growth of the American Bahá'í community, it is interesting to recall that nothing was known of the Bahá'í Faith in the United States until 1893, when the Congress of Religions of the Columbian Exposition gave out some information on it.

Because she was prompted to investigate further into these new teachings in 1897, Mrs. Phoebe Hearst visited the Prison City of 'Akká with other friends, and was able to meet 'Abdu'l-Bahá there.

In 1902 an embryo Bahá'í headquarters was started in Chicago and in their attempts to pattern their lives as closely as possible upon the tenets given in such Bahá'í information as was available at that time, this body finally appealed to 'Abdu'l-Bahá early in the twentieth century for permission to erect a great Temple, a true House of Worship, in the Chicago area. He gave His permission readily.

Much later He wrote: "The continent of America is in the eyes of the one true God, the land wherein the splendors of His light shall be revealed, where the mysteries of His Faith shall be unveiled, where the righteous will abide and the free assemble."

Between that time when there was little knowledge of just how to go about being the kind of people the few Writings from the Faith had hinted were possible, when they had few members, little money, and only a rare dream of spiritual significance, to the present, when the Faith is on so many lips and in so many hearts in all parts of the world as well as in the United States, is a story of such magnificence made up from the determination and individual sacrifice of a dedicated group, that the brief description in these pages will naturally leave much untold. It is meant only to pique the edge of one's interest, and to leave further knowledge until the heart really hungers to know it all.

It was just about the end of World War I, and the world was filled with chaos when Bahá'u'lláh's Faith got its first tiny foothold in Chicago and a few other small areas of America, and all that the uninitiate knew was that it was a religion with worldwide aspirations that had gotten its start and made its initial impact on some Oriental countries.

Certainly, Bahá'u'lláh must have known long before any ideas about a Bahá'í Temple in the West had been started, that there would be this need, for in His Writings, there appear these words:

> O concourse of creation! O people! Construct edifices in the most beautiful fashion possible, in every city, in every land, in the name of the Lord of Religion. Adorn them with that which beseemeth them. Then commemorate the Lord, the Merciful, the Clement, in spirit and in fragrance.

It is not known whether that small initial group of believers in America had ever heard these words, but as their spirit, their dedication, and their determination grew, so did their edifice and the number of followers of the Faith in this country.

The original small group in Chicago was formed in the early 1900s and gradually became the combined National Spiritual Assembly of the United States and Canada. By 1948 the Faith had so grown and developed in the continent of North America that the Guardian asked Canada to organize a national body separate and apart from that of the United States.

The original combined Assembly, however, was the model for all national assemblies that followed. In America the Bahá'ís were always spurred on by the feeling that theirs was a special destiny, and this feeling had been inculcated and fostered by the steady encouragement of first 'Abdu'l-Bahá and then the beloved Guardian.

The cardinal principle followed by Bahá'ís in every country is, of course, the Oneness of Mankind. It places on all believers an obligation far surpassing that of charity and brotherly love. In those parts of America where racial prejudice still tries to prevail, Bahá'ís nevertheless integrate their meetings and local assemblies. No consideration of personal comfort or convenience, material well-being or social status is permitted to stand in the way of applying Bahá'í principle in their conduct and the National Assembly remains always ready to assist a beleaguered Bahá'í group having any sort of difficulty.

A prominent Jewish clergyman, Rabbi Arthur Gilbert, staff consultant of the National Conference of Christians and Jews, has observed that religion in America had become a force of profound significance in a large measure because Americans have had to support the church themselves. Referring to what happened to the church in Germany, he remarked:

> When the church becomes too closely identified with the political order of the society, when it becomes dependent financially on that society, it is bankrupt. It is silent when it should be prophetic.

Bahá'ís point out that Bahá'u'lláh recognized this over a century ago with His warning to Bahá'ís not to become involved in politics and not to solicit or accept funds from any *but* Bahá'ís for their Bahá'í goals and achievements. The initial American believers must have found it very hard to veer from their native background of moral, spiritual, and financial church support.

The material and spiritual growth of the Bahá'í Faith here proves that it can and has been done successfully and without outside appeal or fanfare. Non-Bahá'ís are not importuned for anything but their attendance at Bahá'í meetings, celebrations, and functions, those which are not solely for Bahá'ís, of course.

When non-Bahá'ís plead to contribute financially to the Bahá'í funds, they are advised first that such money is used only for special charitable purposes.

By the time the dream of the first American believers became concrete enough to invite 'Abdu'l-Bahá to dedicate the cornerstone of the planned Temple in Wilmette, Illinois, there were still only the barest beginnings both spiritually and financially to what was eventually to become a giant stronghold of the Faith in North America. Few of them imagined that within thirty or forty years they would not only have their magnificent edifice standing as a monument to their spiritual dedication, but that the Faith in America would send its followers out into the far reaches of the world and help the teachings to spread where they had never even been anticipated before.

As an idea of the progress of the Bahá'í work in the United States, the annual report given to the believers at their 1965 national convention included the following information:

There had been more nationwide publicity of the Faith that year than in any year of its history, including stories in national magazines, syndicated newspaper columns, on radio and on television.

There had been many, many new believers enrolled and twenty-nine percent of the newcomers were youths, meaning between fifteen and twenty-one years of age.

The American states recognizing Bahá'í legal marriages to be solemnized by incorporated local Spiritual Assemblies had reached a total of thirty-eight. And recognition of Bahá'í Holy Days by communities in which Bahá'ís lived in the United States had reached one hundred and ten and there were signs already of higher figures within a short time.

Many schools in the United States now permit Bahá'ís to take time off for their Holy Days, and the believers are also acquainting business people with the validity of time off for their religious holidays, just as is done for those of other faiths.

The American Bahá'í community reported that it had accepted

the responsibility for establishing Bahá'í Institutions in other areas of the North American continent, particularly the Caribbean, and by the beginning of the year 1966, these Caribbean goals had already been reached. American Bahá'í teachers were being sent to other foreign areas, also, to help them achieve their own goals of increased Bahá'í memberships everywhere that is was spiritually possible.

As the National Assembly of the Bahá'ís of the United States also has the duty to enforce American Bahá'í marriage and divorce laws, to concern itself with governmental relationships and to adjudicate many personal matters in the life of the membership, it reported that the number of such problems had increased and that plans were being worked up to help local Bahá'í communities and individual Bahá'ís, themselves, to share more of this responsibility under national administrative guidance.

The Bahá'í Publishing Trust, which puts out the pamphlets and Bahá'í Writings and materials used in Bahá'í teaching work, had now become self-sustaining and in 1965 had sold nearly $100,000 worth of such printed materials. Considering that these sales are through Bahá'í outlets only, not through commercial bookstores, outside sales representatives or even regular advertising outlets, unless a Local Assembly wishes to do something like this with national approval, this is truly a noteworthy accomplishment.

In 1965, as in the other years from its inception, the National Assembly in the United States had supervised the work and personnel of numerous committees that were part of its work in spurring on the teaching of the Faith.

All committee activities are supervised, created, and fostered through the National Assembly in some way. The printed annual report of these many activities consumed twenty-four printed pages, and has grown progressively bulkier each year.

Nevertheless, nothing the American believers do or have done can match the drama, intensity, and effectiveness that has been displayed by them in the erection of their Bahá'í House of Worship at Wilmette, which thereupon deserves considerable special mention in this volume.

The Wilmette Properties

THE PERSIAN NAME for the Bahá'í House of Worship is Mash-riqu'l-Adhkár, which literally means "The Dawning-Place of the Remembrance of God."

The Bahá'í hope is that eventually every Bahá'í center will include a building set apart for God's work, and have around it such institutions built by the Bahá'ís as a hospice, a hospital, a school of science, a home for the aged and a home for the orphaned.

The central building or place of worship for Bahá'ís is to be compared with the heart or innermost point of illumination, according to Bahá'í description, and those buildings surrounding it would symbolize the good works performed in the name of the Manifestation. Within the place of worship people of all races and beliefs will find inspiration and the surrounding institutions will express this inspiration to the world through loving service to humanity.

The tract of land for the Wilmette Temple was acquired in 1908 and the completed structure was publicly dedicated in the spring of 1953. The entire project cost nearly $3 million, including the landscaping and terrace, and its construction was inspired by the original Bahá'í building in Turkestan, once part of the Persian Empire. It was eventually razed by the Russians.

The architect of the Wilmette Temple was a Frenchman, a non-Bahá'í whose design was selected from six different ones offered. He had conceived a Temple of Light in which the structure was so uniquely worked out as to be concealed, with visible supports eliminated, when possible. The effect was intended to be that of a lacy envelope enshrining a spiritual idea.

The significance of this design was described by the architect, whose name was Louis Bourgeois:

The teachings of Bahá'u'lláh unify the religions of the world into one universal religion, and as we know that all great historic religions developed a new architecture, so the Bahá'í Temple is the plastic teachings of Bahá'u'lláh. In the Bahá'í Temple is used a composite architecture, expressing the essence in line of each of the great architectural styles, harmonizing them into one whole.

Mr. Bourgeois for years had been working on designs for the Temple of Peace at The Hague, but nothing had satisfied him. One night he had a vision that so moved him he had to get up and make some sketches of a nine-sided building with minarets at the corners. The only part of the vision that came to him at first was the two stories.

For three months he was stymied and failed to progress far enough to at least satisfy himself. One morning in a flash of light he saw the dome of the building. It was *on* the building. He made a quick sketch of the entire structure and dome on a piece of wrapping paper, then went back to sleep. When he looked at his creation in the morning he realized that it was something so new and different that trying to put it into blueprint form would not do justice to the originality of the idea. He had to make a plaster model of his unusual concept!

The building is nine-sided. All of the sides are alike, with a doorway at the center, flanked on either side by two ornamental windows and enclosed with a flat arch. The sides are curved and concave, symbolizing the architect's concept of extending outstretched arms. The first story is thirty-six feet high, on a circular foundation with nineteen steps from the ground surface up to the main floor. A second story of forty-five feet is considerably recessed, again with nine sides, each having a group of windows. Above is the clerestory, nineteen feet to the dome, which rises a little over two hundred feet above the ground.

The building's nine sides are most unique and the fact that the second story is offset in reference to the first caused considerable comment from the very first time the design was exhibited. The architect felt he had introduced a new principle in design by making the ribs curved to abut against the arched faces of the building. When he tried to change this to have the ribs and the minarets of the first gallery in line with the pylons of the first story, the whole design became lifeless and he was forced to return to his original concept.

The nine ribs which extend over the dome terminate in a point on top, seeming to symbolize hands lifted in prayer.

Visitors who study the geometric forms of the ornamentation, which cover the columns and surrounding windows and doors of the building, can decipher thereon the religious symbols of the world. The nine-pointed star reappears as the Bahá'í symbol time and again in the formation of the windows and doors, from which extended gilded rays cover the lower surfaces and seem to illustrate vividly and artistically the descent of the Holy Spirit.

To Bahá'ís the number nine also signifies perfection or completion, and since there is no digit higher than 9, it and 19 recur many times in the Temple as an illustration of the basic Bahá'í principle of Unity. Nine contains in itself the completion of each perfect number cycle and nineteen represents the Union of God and man, in life, civilization, and all things.

The building work of the Temple began in 1921 with the foundation construction. By 1929 the Trustees had received enough cash donations from the believers to proceed with the building of the superstructure during the following year.

Just as this project started, however, Louis Bourgeois died in his studio home on the Temple property, but he had already completed his design, including full-sized drawings of remarkable beauty and accuracy of all the exterior ornamentation. Some of these drawings actually reached a length of 109 feet.

Over a period of nine years many painstaking details had to be worked out, so that everything would fit perfectly into the design as the brushstrokes of the master painter fit into and form a part of his masterpiece. It might have been easier if the architect had still been alive, but it could not have achieved greater perfection after the ordeal was ended.

Always there were delays before the work could proceed to its next step, not only because of the difficulty in raising the funds necessary from this infant Bahá'í community, but because many of the materials used had to be created for their special effect, and actually brought new ideas to the construction industry. Since the Bahá'í membership in America was small, it should be emphasized, and no contributions could be accepted from non-Bahá'ís, it became a matter of great individual sacrifice to keep the funds flowing, and the American believers were indeed grateful that Bahá'ís from everywhere looked upon this as their Temple, also, and helped with their own contributions.

In addition, during Shoghi Effendi's Seven-Year Teaching Plan, the Guardian had cautioned the believers that their first responsibility was to raise funds for teaching and other administrative expenses and it became a matter of real struggle to the American community to obey by taking care of first things first, and then raising the building funds, afterwards.

However, obey they did and with radiant acquiescence.

By July 1939, not only had the nine faces of the building been completed, but so had the pouring of the cement for the nine pylons and their capitals. The Bahá'ís knew that urgency was the motto of the day, because of the rapidly spreading World War II conditions and the possibility of restrictions in building materials.

Nevertheless the work of the preliminary steps for the main story ornamentation was accomplished so expediently and well that the cost for this was $10,000 less than the original $50,000 estimate.

The involvement, finally, of the United States in the world fracas and the curtailment, as expected, of the use of essential building materials in nonwar building activities proved the wisdom of their own advance acquisition of the materials needed.

One could become quite repetitious listing the new complications, other financial hurdles, and ever-rising difficulties, all of which were overcome, so that by 1942 things looked like clear sailing ahead, until the War and Navy departments entered into contracts with the contractor who was supposed to work on the ornamentation, and it then appeared that the insurmountable hurdle had finally been approached. Miraculously it hadn't! In some way the contractor managed to eke out one foreman with two assistants as a Temple labor force, and not only the main-story ornamentation but the steps were well under way by the middle of May 1942.

Of course the project, which had long been regarded as impracticable by architects, engineers, builders, and others who had inspected the original plaster model, became a marvel of enduring concrete, steel, and other materials by the time the entire building was ready for occupancy. Never before in the history of building construction had so many new ideas been developed to meet a need, and so many new techniques of construction been evolved, as well as so many problems solved in both labor and ingenuity.

The final composition was a beautiful structure on a huge triangle of land located in the center of a six-acre tract. Its glistening, white quartz-concrete ornamentation, its high dome rising 165 feet above the surrounding landscape, is an imposing picture from all directions around and over it, and has become a beacon to Lake Michigan navigation as well as the air traffic overhead.

The gardens marked the culmination of nearly half a century of a sacrifice and labor to the American believers. There are nine of them, each differently designed, each nestled into the arms of the incurving terrace section of the Temple. The rhythm of the alternating curved faces of the structure appears carried into the garden setting with appropriate gradation. There are steps and walks and approaches, there are clipped yew hedges and rows of columnar Chinese junipers along either side. As one enters an approach the picture of the entrance façade enframed with the avenue junipers are deliberately reminiscent of the Orient.

The problem of illuminating the exterior of the Temple and providing at least a "moonlight glow" lighting in the gardens and along approaches was studied by landscape specialists and finally conquered with unique hedges and garden arrangements. Areas beyond this outer circle were treated as a parklike setting of shrub-bordered and tree-studded lawns.

The entire effect is a landscape setting of restraint, dignity, and matchless beauty. Over ten years have passed since it was completed, and now the matured plants, the developed trees lend their lovely design in such a way that together with the Temple building itself it is breathtaking to view, even in a color photograph.

Only a short while after the completion of the Temple, with its offices laid out in the basement for some of the Bahá'í work, a separate building was constructed nearby for the expanded Bahá'í Publishing Trust activities, plus still another for the National Offices. The huge house across the street from the House of Worship, once the administrative offices, is now primarily used for the residence of the National Secretary, and as the meeting place for the National Assembly.

In 1963 the first of the social service buildings came into being and use. It is the Bahá'í Home for the Aged, with reasonable rates and excellent accommodations for Bahá'ís and non-Bahá'ís who, in the twilight of their lives, need a loving, comfortable atmosphere.

The National Assembly has for a long while issued a monthly *Bahá'í News* in two sections, one that is purely of American Bahá'í interest, the other with international items along the Bahá'í front. Now, after a hiatus of many years there has been announced the resumption of publication of the Bahá'í magazine, *World Order,* to feature material of broad intellectual, theological, cultural, and human interest by both Bahá'í and other authors, for an audience of broad literary tastes, and not merely to expound Bahá'í concerns.

In 1965 the Bahá'í Publishing Trust quarters were enlarged again, and the national offices had further mushroomed into temporary rented space until a decision could be made whether to construct more buildings at this time.

Small wonder that twenty-four hours a day do not seem enough time for the Wilmette workers. Promulgating a Faith that has grown as rapidly as the Bahá'í Cause has since 'Abdu'l-Bahá visited the United States in 1912 is something that cannot be done on a nine-to-five, five-days-a-week basis, without counting upon a two-week vacation. There are no such things as real vacations among those who toil in Bahá'í vineyards. They seek to raise a crop in every season.

The Work of the Wilmette House of Worship

ANNUALLY the total number of visitors to this edifice is well over 100,000 people, which figures increases with each passing year. There are people who visit it and have to go out of their way from Chicago to do so, as it is approximately an hour's ride by public transportation or car between Chicago and Wilmette. Many visitiors have heard of the Temple in other parts of the world, and go to Chicago especially to see it. It is therefore, unlike the usual "tourist attaction," made easily available to reach.

During the tourist season from May through October, the Temple's Foundation Hall area has exhibits, displays, a book counter, and an auditorium where a slide program narration on the Faith is available for visitors. The whole building upstairs requires five Bahá'í volunteers at all times, or a total of fifty-five man-hours covered each day. It is staffed by local and visiting believers who spend their free time giving such service. These hosts and hostesses welcome all visitors, answer hundreds of inquiries from those hearing of the Faith for the first time, and direct others to points of interest at a guided pace suited to individual needs.

There are also hundreds of special tours scheduled through the

Temple each year, many for groups holding conventions in Chicago. Other groups from nearby areas are from other religious affiliations, high-school classes, universities, sight-seeing bus tours, senior citizens clubs, National Conference of Christians and Jews, and foreign students from all parts of the world who visit there under the auspices of such organizations as the American Field Service, the World Assembly of Youth and others.

Thousands of pieces of free Bahá'í literature are given out at the Temple and many thousands more are mailed out in response to requests seeking further information on the teachings.

In addition to the regularly scheduled weekly devotional programs held each Sunday, and the public meetings held on every Sunday, there are special Bahá'í programs commemorating their Holy Days and special events days, as well as meetings and receptions for various distinguished Bahá'í visitors from all parts of the universe and the States.

Memorial services are held for deceased Bahá'ís of note, and a fellowship hour for children takes place each week. Occasionally, nonpolitical or nonreligious gatherings take place there of groups whose aims and goals reflect one or more of the Bahá'í principles of service to mankind, such as the World Federalists, United Nations, League of Women Voters, and Human Relations Councils.

Each year the local incorporated Bahá'í Assemblies near the Temple area witness the exchange of marriage vows of various couples. These weddings are held in the Temple gardens, in Foundation Hall, or in the smaller reception room, giving the Bahá'ís an additional opportunity to demonstrate their beliefs to guests of other religious backgrounds, whenever the marriages were of a Bahá'í to another religious exponent.

There are weekly programs of devotion and *a cappella* music in the Auditorium of the House of Worship. The selection of choral numbers, as well as of choral singers, is a precise and rewarding effort that pleases the multitudes who come to hear the music as well as the program of readings from the Writings of all the world Faiths.

The National Spiritual Assembly of the Bahá'ís of the United States begins each of its regular meetings with morning prayers in the House of Worship. This spiritually strengthens the members for the burdens that have been placed upon their hearts, their souls, and their consciences by the delegates who elected them at the annual national convention.

The nine inscriptions from Bahá'u'lláh's Writings over each arch of the main doorways remind all who come that the Bahá'í beliefs are truly a part of other people's religious heritage:

"The earth is but one country, and mankind its citizens."

"The best beloved of all things in My sight is Justice; turn not away therefrom if thou desirest Me."

"My love is My stronghold; he that entereth therein is safe and secure."

"Breathe not the sins of others so long as thou art thyself a sinner."

"Thy heart is My home; sanctify it for My descent."

"I have made death a messenger of joy to thee; wherefore dost thou grieve?"

"Make mention of Me on My earth that in My heaven I may remember thee."

"O Rich ones on earth! The poor in your midst are My trust; guard ye My Trust."

"The source of all learning is the knowledge of God, exalted be His glory."

Actually the Hidden Words of Bahá'u'lláh are not hidden. They were called "hidden" because all through the centuries their content was unknown until Bahá'u'lláh revealed them. Just as they are engraved over each arch of the main doorways of the American Bahá'í Temple, so are they engraved upon the hearts and deeds of all the true believers.

The Path of
the True Believer

The Bahá'í Meaning of "Love"

ONE OF THE MOST difficult things for a new Bahá'í to accept is the use of the word "love" in everything his fellow believers say and do. It's very hard for someone to differentiate at first between the physical form of "love" prevalent in the mundane world, and the spiritual form of it evidenced by the Bahá'ís in action.

Not that the Bahá'ís individually may appear to be any more "lovable" than one's non-Bahá'í neighbor or non-Bahá'í relative. It is in concert that their expression of "love" is most evident, when they are striving together to worship, work, and live in the Bahá'í way.

What *is* the Bahá'í way? It's a selfless one that removes personal considerations from individual action. For example, before declaring one's self, the sensitive person might take casual remarks to be pointed or critical. After being around the believers he learns to look for their motive first, and if he cannot find it to be as pure as it should, then he must look within himself for forgiveness and forgetfulness of whatever may have seemed wrong in the other person.

The path of the true believer may seem thorny to the untrained eye. It is based upon the qualities difficult to achieve of obedience, acceptance, prayer, and love. Ah . . . there's that word again—

love! It's something that butters a Bahá'í's bread, enriches his heart, fills his soul, and gives meaning to everything in his life, because he knows that he and his Bahá'í "family," whatever their faults, have one thing in common, which few other groups have. They have the Message for this Day, they have the "prescription," and even if they fail to follow the directions exactly at least they're all in this "trying" procedure together. And . . . out of this trying, this striving, this sacrificing, this learning, there comes a pure love that eventually is far more concerned with how to help the other person than in what that person can do for the Bahá'í friend.

The goal of all Bahá'ís is to achieve the Kingdom of God here on earth, and each one quickly learns that this can't be done alone. In fact, if he wanted to be alone, the seeker would not have become a Bahá'í in the first place.

There is nothing like the joy of approval from people who have discovered the good in someone else. That's where the "look for the good, not for the bad" motto comes into play with the Bahá'ís. They actually do seek ways to love, to express joy, to bring laughter and light and courage to each other, and they also find ways to bring light into darkness and understanding into sadness or suffering, when either of these is needed.

The true Bahá'í learns that without one of those hard-to-acquire qualities, the others are never as effective, and without any of them at all he would be unable to understand or to progress towards the other Worlds of God.

Obedience, of course, doesn't always include automatic understanding of what one is obedient to, but in the Faith it means to follow the administrative teachings and the spiritual writings. Each believer learns that once he acquires obedience to these principles—all predicated upon the Writings of Bahá'u'lláh, incidentally—that he acquires an objective form of "love," as well, since one cannot hate that which gives him an inner glow, the way doing the "right" thing and following the right path always does.

Being obedient is another way of finding out the difference between rigid discipline and consultative decision. Bahá'ís are never *forced* to do the unacceptable, but in becoming Bahá'ís they accept the innate, divine guidance of the principles, the administration, and the laws given them to follow. In the Faith they find that freedom of thought and the privilege of obedience are actually blended. They endeavor to make use of such freedom according to the laws of Bahá'í administration.

The believer doesn't argue because his ideas aren't accepted. He freely "gives" his opinions or suggestions to counselors, and then learns to go his way happily, whether or not they are used. From then on he is free for his most important obligations:

1. To be firm in the Covenant of Bahá'u'lláh . . . and to love.

2. To display and feel love and unity . . . and to give love, as well.

3. To teach the Faith to others . . . and with love.

Again "love" is the emollient to make all else go smoothly in the Bahá'í life. If the believer feels love for the Faith, love for his Bahá'í brothers and sisters and love for Bahá'u'lláh, he can accept whatever God wills for him and do it humbly, not for praise or self-aggrandizement. If he loves, and then if he is humble, he learns that his spirit will become stronger for the vicissitudes that will surely come. And these vicissitudes or "tests," as Bahá'ís call them, are what they are most certain of, because they are taught that only through the struggle to win over tests can a Bahá'í win over himself and do things for God, rather than for glory.

Whatever disappointments occur, the true believer knows he will become reinforced gradually against pettiness and pain, and that eventually he too may become a receptacle for others from which will pour forth all the beauty of Bahá'í love, friendship, and accomplishment.

He realizes that because of the lack of love and humility among people, groups or nations there develop crises and the weakening of the Divine Power which causes God to send mankind a new Prophet and a new Message. He knows that such

Prophets come again and again to this earth to bring love and unity to its peoples, and that all Divine Manifestations have been united in this Mission and Purpose.

"Beware, O believers in the Unity of God," the true believer reads, "lest ye be tempted to make any distinction between any of the Manifestations of His Cause, or to discriminate against the signs that have accompanied their Revelation. . . ."

The Bahá'í Meaning of Worship, Work, and Humility

The true believer learns to acquire humility for the sake of God, not for himself. He learns that without humility he cannot live with his fellow citizens, be they Bahá'ís or not, because without it he cannot learn the Bahá'í spirit of unity, justice, and truth.

The true believer in an attitude of humility seeks to attain a pure heart. He knows that whatever problems may rain down upon him, they will help to develop his spiritual capacities. He does not perform good deeds to preen himself or to rest upon such laurels. When he is truly humble, he will not believe his kindness, generosity, or friendliness are anything but basic qualities to be used for others, although he fervently prays and hopes that whatever he possesses will be used to demonstrate the best traditions of his Faith.

He achieves much of this strength and spiritual guidance through constant study of the Bahá'í Writings and especially through prayer. There is a daily obligatory prayer and other special prayers, each intended to bring him a divine channel to God. The true believer learns that to pray wisely and well is to listen with an open heart in an attempt to "hear" God's answer. Through 'Abdu'l-Bahá's wisdom he finds "the worshiper must pray with a detached spirit, unconditional surrender of the will, concentrated attention and spiritual passion," that prayer is not the reading of words or fidgeting for a required number of minutes. It is making no demands upon God, asking only for His love.

The true believer finds that the work he does in the form of service and with love is also a form of prayer. All Bahá'ís are required to engage in useful occupation and to try to be self-supporting. They are asked to meet their personal obligations and to attend to the needs of their families.

Bahá'ís are supposed to be joyous under all conditions, to accept graciously, not grudgingly, whatever demands Bahá'u'lláh may make of them. Despite 'Abdu'l-Bahá's many years of imprisonment, He always smiled at those around Him, and never failed to be concerned for others, or to ask, "Are you happy? Are you happy?"

In the Bahá'í Writings, He states: "Though I stay in prison, it is just like paradise; afflictions and trials in the path of God give me joy; troubles rest me; death is life; to be despised is honor ... Seek, O servant of God, this life until day and night you remain in limitless joy."

Therefore the true believer does his job or any other task as pleasantly as possible, trying not to resent something foreign to his likes, or different from what he expected. When the situation can be changed, he has confidence that Bahá'u'lláh will help it to be easier, but until then that is where the "acceptance" comes in.

Bahá'ís are human beings, of course, and most human beings are not easily taught to become joyous despite pain, poverty, or personal loneliness. Therefore, again, the true believer does not complain of his life or associations, he will mention only their positive side, if he mentions them at all, and he will endeavor to be a joy to those around him.

The key to all this is the Bahá'í idea of love. Each Bahá'í learns to express his love for God through prayer and through his attitude toward his fellow man. Bahá'í love is a divine, selfless, and unlimited love. It needs no reciprocity, it needs only to be needed in order to shower itself upon others. It is not fawning, obvious, or used in such a way that others are uncomfortable because of it. It is a warming glow that permeates the surroundings, the deeds, the thoughts of the Bahá'í expressing such love. It is indeed a jewel that dangles before each one, and only sincerity, humility, and selfless desire can achieve it.

The true believer tries not to hurt, criticize, or belittle anyone else. This is part of the divine quality of his love for others. If he must point out an inaccuracy, he will do it so lovingly that it appears the fault is his own, so that the other will not feel he is being blamed. If the true believer is treated badly by someone, he returns only love, not argument or reproach and eventually, it is hoped, will forget the reason for hurt.

'Abdu'l-Bahá expressed this quality frequently of "turning the other cheek." When His worst enemies would revile Him, He would treat them as though they were His closest friends. Only if they tried to hurt the Cause of God would He then turn away from them completely. When they merely tried to hurt Him it was as though nothing had happened because He knew that pure, selfless love can turn the worst enemy into a repentant friend. He has passed this knowledge on in His Writings.

Bahá'í love is very openly expressed at Nineteen-Day Feasts or other Bahá'í gatherings. These embraces are things of pure joy, an expression of delight in being reunited and pressed close to the heart of someone else, someone who is very precious because he is a Bahá'í friend.

The Bahá'í Meaning of the Soul, and the Hereafter

WHEN YOU ASK a Bahá'í if he believes in another existence beyond this earthly one, he often presents the analogy of the child struggling in the womb of the mother and not wanting to enter this world. If that infant knew the joys which now await him, the believer explains, he might not struggle, he would never be afraid to leave that comfortable shell in which he developed for nine months.

The same is true when the believers contemplate what is commonly thought of as Death. To a Bahá'í, life is a continuing journey through all the Worlds of God, and after he leaves this world he fully expects to continue to still another.

To a Bahá'í, death is not ceasing to exist. It is an exit from an outer shell to something far different, far more wonderful than man has ever known or contemplated. Bahá'u'lláh has written:

> If any man be told that which hath been ordained for such a soul in the worlds of God, the Lord of the throne on high and of earth below, his whole being will instantly blaze out in his great longing to attain that most exalted, that sanctified and resplendent station. . . .

In the same context, the Bahá'ís do not believe in Heaven or Hell as places, but as conditions. 'Abdu'l-Bahá has written that to be in heaven is to "move in the atmosphere of God's Holy Will." Therefore, to the believer the condition of Hell is the probable condition of Godlessness or of being without hope for continuation of His love.

Thus we come to the Bahá'í concept of the soul. At the time of birth, the Bahá'ís are taught, the soul is like a bud waiting to grow and flower. Through each person's deeds—good or bad—the soul is either improved or retarded in its growth. Bahá'u'lláh has also written:

> Know, verily, that the soul is a sign of God, a heavenly gem whose reality the most learned of men hath failed to grasp and whose mystery no mind, however acute, can ever hope to unravel. It is the first thing among all created things to declare the excellence of its Creator. . . . If it be faithful to God, it will reflect His light, and will, eventually, return unto Him.

In addition He states:

> Consider the rational faculty with which God hath endowed the essence of man. Examine thine own self, and behold how thy motion and stillness, thy will and purpose, thy sight and hearing, thy sense of smell and power of speech, and whatever else is related to, or transcendeth, thy physical senses or spirit-

ual perceptions, all proceed from, and owe their existence to, this same faculty . . . which should be regarded as a Sign of the revelation of Him Who is the sovereign Lord of all.

Upon the reality of man, however, He hath focused the radiance of all His names and attributes, and made it a mirror of His own self.

The soul of man is the sun by which his body is illumined, and from which it draweth its sustenance, and should be so regarded.

Time and again Bahá'u'lláh has taught that the full nature of the soul is neither describable nor possible to be described:

The nature of the soul after death can never be described, nor is it meet and permissible to reveal its whole character to the eyes of men.

Among the verses of the New Testament regarding the immortality of life are the following: "God spake unto him [Moses] saying I am the God of Abraham, and the God of Isaac and the God of Jacob. He is not the God of the dead but of the living." Also, ". . . this is life eternal, that they might know thee, the one true God, and Jesus Christ, whom thou hast sent."

'Abdu'l-Bahá explains:

According to natural philosophy it is an assured fact that single or simple elements are indestructible. . . . If an elementary substance is possessed of immortality, how can the human spirit or reality, which is wholly above combination and composition, be destroyed?

And still again:

As the spirit of man is not composed of material elements, it is not subject to decomposition and therefore has no death.

In His Writings, 'Abdu'l-Bahá also explains some of Bahá'u'-lláh's other expositions on the soul:

When we speak of the soul we mean the motive power of this physical body which lives until its entire control in accordance with its dictates. . . . There is, however, a faculty in

man which unfolds to his vision the secrets of existence. . . .
This is the power of the mind, for the soul is not, of itself,
capable of unrolling the mysteries of phenomena; but the
mind can accomplish this. . . . There is still another power
which is differentiated from that of the soul and mind . . . it
is the effulgence of the sun of reality. . . . The spirit is the
axis round which the eternal life revolves.

Also:

The soul acts in the physical world with the help of the
body. When it is freed from the body it acts without an intermediary.

Explaining the connection of the soul with the body, 'Abdu'l-
Bahá states:

. . . Though the soul is a resident of the body it is not to be
found in the body. When man dies, his relation with body
ceases. The sun is reflected in the mirror. . . . If the mirror be
broken the sun does not die. The body is the temporary
mirror; the spiritual soul suffers no change, no more than the
sun does.

And further, He says:

. . . Unlike the animal, man has a rational soul, the human
intelligence. This intelligence of man is the intermediary between his body and his spirit. When man allows the spirit,
through his soul, to enlighten his understanding, then does he
contain all creation. . . . Illumined by the spirit through the
instrumentality of the soul, man's radiant intelligence makes
him the crowning-point of creation.

The Bahá'ís do not doubt that there is a purpose for all created
things and that all are moving towards the fulfillment of that
purpose or destiny. Regarding human destiny, Bahá'u'lláh writes:

Know thou of a truth that the soul, after its separation from
the body, will continue to progress until it attaineth the presence of God. . . . It will endure as long as the Kingdom of
God, His sovereignty, His dominion and power will endure.
. . . The Prophets and Messengers of God have been sent down
for the sole purpose of guiding mankind to the straight Path

of Truth . . . to educate all men, that they may, at the hour of death, ascend, in the utmost purity and sanctity and with absolute detachment, to the throne of the most High.

Just before 'Abdu'l-Bahá was to sail away from America a woman came to Him, admitting her fear of death.

"Then," He said, "do something that will keep you from dying; that will instead, day by day, make you more alive, and bring you everlasting life. According to the words of His Holiness Christ, those who enter the Kingdom of God will never die. Then enter the Divine Kingdom, and fear death no more."

The true believer accepts that human destiny is eventual joyous reunion with God. Bahá'u'lláh assures, "I have made Death a Messenger of joy to thee; wherefore dost thou grieve?"

The Bahá'ís believe that the human soul will continue to live through all the Worlds of God and that the path to reunion with Him is through following His precepts and learning to love and serve and worship Him.

The Command to Teach the Faith

AS SOON AS a Bahá'í is declared, he has the command to teach. There is no need for the new believer to wait until he has become an accomplished scholar of the Teachings. He can use those things he learned for declaring himself, as a start. Those who cannot give lectures are asked to teach by example or are urged to introduce their new beliefs to friends by inviting them to attend Bahá'í lectures and activities.

Bahá'u'lláh has stated in this regard:

"Whosoever quickens one soul in this Cause is like unto one quickening all the servants and the Lord shall bring him forth in the day of the resurrection. . . ."

Bahá'u'lláh has also said: "No act, however great, can compare with it. . . ." "Such a service [teaching] is, indeed, the prince of all goodly deeds and the ornament of every goodly act. . . ."

'Abdu'l-Bahá has stipulated and encouraged teaching:

> It is known and clear that today the unseen divine assistance
> encompasseth those who deliver the Message. And if the work
> of delivering the Message be neglected, the assistance shall
> be entirely cut off, for it is impossible that the friends of God
> could receive assistance unless they be engaged in delivering
> the Message.

Shoghi Effendi considered teaching so important that (as previously mentioned herein) on one occasion he wrote explicitly to the American believers that it even overshadowed the building of their Wilmette Temple and, as the Bahá'ís would teach and spread the Cause, the many new souls coming into the Faith would make possible the continuance of the Temple work.

The Guardian stressed over and over again that to effectively teach the Faith the individual had to deeply study the Divine Word. He should then meditate on the import of the Word, and after finding its spiritual depths he should pray for guidance and assistance. The Guardian then instructed that after prayer there should be action, along with wisdom and audacity, and Bahá'í teachers have found that the combination of these have proved most successful.

The believers are taught that there can be no limit to their continual study of the Teachings. No matter how much a Bahá'í has learned there are always new ideas being offered in study seminars and teaching institutes that are frequently prepared for American Bahá'í communities under the auspices of the National Spiritual Assembly by the National Teaching Committee, a sub-division of their National Goals Committee.

Teaching efforts for non-Bahá'ís take two forms. One is the fireside method of talks in private homes, which Bahá'ís attend or to which they bring along friends they know. The expanded version of this is the public meeting in a hall hired for the occasion, or a Bahá'í Center, which can be a regular basis or for special occasions and is announced through advertisements and other publicity methods.

Experienced teachers of the Faith can become pioneers or

traveling Bahá'í teachers at home or abroad, and they are inspired frequently by the Words of Bahá'u'lláh which 'Abdu'l-
Bahá quoted in His "Tablets of the Divine Plan" for America:

> If they arise to teach My Cause they must let the Breath of
> Him Who is unconstrained stir them and must spread It abroad
> on the earth with high resolve, with minds that are wholly
> centered in Him and with hearts that are completely detached
> from and independent of all things and with souls that are
> sanctified from the world and its vanities. It behooveth them to
> choose as the best provision for their journey reliance upon
> God and to clothe themselves with the Love of their Lord,
> the Most Exalted, the All-Glorious. If they do so, their words
> shall influence their hearers. . . .
>
> By the Righteousness of God should a man all alone rise
> in the Name of Bahá and put on the Armor of His Love, him
> will the Almighty cause to be victorious though the Forces
> of Heaven and Hell be arrayed against him. . . .

A Bahá'í pioneer is usually self-supporting, and travels wherever his teaching services are needed. He can start a Bahá'í stronghold, increase the numbers in a group and help make it into an
Assembly, or reinforce an Assembly that is in danger of losing its
status through the loss by death or the moving away of a member
or two. Once a pioneer's services have helped to increase the
membership in a goal community, he then becomes available
either to pioneer elsewhere or to return home, whichever he
chooses.

Bahá'ís are quick to point out that the rising number of their
believers in the United States is due to certain important reasons,
reasons that are beyond the implicit value of the teachings themselves. One is that these teachings are modern, that older religious
teachings have been rejuvenated, another that this Faith is the
most timely. In America, people are interested in social issues and
to the Bahá'ís education and the spiritual solution to economic
problems are an intrinsic part of their Faith.

Bahá'í teachers are patient, they take time to answer someone's
questions, except political questions that have a tinge which

necessitates reference to administrative channels. Years ago, people received their religious philosophy through its being passed on by their families. Today people are maturing. When they take the time to investigate truth, to ask questions, they learn how exciting it can be to live during the Bahá'í Era, whether or not they ever join its ranks for themselves.

The believers emphasize that in the Bahá'í Writings the North American continent "is to be a cradle of the new world order," and that this is to demonstrate without any question that from all the crass materialism which now exists there can still be expected to rise up a race of spiritual beings. When that happens, which they feel *can* happen by living under the Bahá'í banner, it will be one example of the power of their Faith which the world will be able to understand and accept.

Bahá'í teachers are intended to be examples of the Bahá'í principles in action. In the United States this is through integration.

Until April 1963, for instance, a small city in Illinois had no Negro residents and its citizens generally wanted none. Through a firm stand taken by the local believers and their Spiritual Assembly, the prejudiced atmosphere finally changed to one of understanding and respect for the Bahá'í principles.

It was just about that time that the Local Assembly was threatened by the dwindling of its community to seven believers. Three Bahá'ís planned to resettle there. One of these was a Negro. They knew the violent opposition that could possibly develop from a Negro moving to what was intended as an all-white community; an Assembly member was delegated to meet with the city's Mayor who, in turn, gave permission for the "move-in" on the grounds that it was a religiously motivated plan. The Mayor made it clear, however, that integration on any other basis would be difficult and without the benefit of his civic office.

The white couple arrived and made early contact with a neighbor to discuss the impending arrangement. This neighbor, greatly upset, telephoned the Mayor, who visited the new couple and realized they were two of the three involved in the "move-in" that he had approved. He spoke of the implications and was assured that the Bahá'ís were fully aware of possible negative reactions, and he then requested a letter stating the full circumstances so that it could be used as a protection against possible malicious gossip.

The Mayor further suggested that the Negro Bahá'í delay his arrival for another week, until the Mayor had contacted local ministers and other influential sympathizers. This same Mayor also planned various protective measures for the Bahá'ís, including hourly squad car surveillance of the area.

As requested, the Local Spiritual Assembly wrote to the Mayor, giving the reason for the new inhabitants coming there, their educational, business, and professional backgrounds, their teaching and other Bahá'í services, as well as the Negro Baha'í's attendance at the Bahá'í World Congress in London that year. The letter concluded:

"Mr. ———— and Mr. and Mrs. ———— did not come to ———— as Negro and Caucasians, but as Bahá'ís, and as such, accept binding upon their own individual and inner lives the following words." These words by 'Abdu'l-Bahá called for rectitude of conduct, love, kindliness, good will, and friendliness, as well as the banishment of ignorance, enmity, hate, and rancor.

The following Sunday the Mayor personally picked up the letter and four days later a four-page letter signed by the Mayor, quoting the Assembly's missive in full, was sent to some two hundred citizens of that city. He warned that rumors and any untoward actions against the Bahá'ís would create potential danger to all homes in the area and stated that it was his (the Mayor's) intention to execute the responsibilities of his office in maintaining the public health, welfare, and safety of all citizens there.

The immediate reaction was heart-warming and far surpassed the fondest hopes of the Bahá'ís in that community. Various civic groups, church dignitaries, and others contacted them, inviting them to participate in community or special activities, and the Negro Bahá'í was invited to give a book review for the League of Women Voters when he arrived there to live. This meeting was publicized in the local paper.

The Bahá'í community soon held a reception for those who had expressed interest and good wishes, and among those attending were the Mayor and other prominent and influential citizens of the city, including a Catholic priest who had initially been most cordial in seeking them out. There has been nothing but warmth and friendliness for the Bahá'ís in that area since then, and their teaching work is progressing well.

In October 1963 a Negro member of the police force of a small Utah city was gunned down trying to apprehend an escapee from a state institution. He left a widow, three children, and his mother without funds to face the future. Worried about this, a member of the Bahá'í community there, without much encouragement from any persons except other Bahá'ís, launched a drive for funds, raising several thousand dollars from individuals, organizations, and firms in Utah, which were to be presented to the bereaved family that Christmas.

Although there was little appreciable cooperation from the majority of the populace, since there was a general deep-seated prejudice against Negroes in the state, the Bahá'í leader of the drive publicly thanked those, including the Governor of Utah, who supported her efforts. At the same time she pointed out that everyone needed to be genuinely concerned about settling so cheaply this account of one who "had great faith and pride in his community and performed his job of dedication beyond the call of duty."

Commenting upon the community's responsiveness, the Bahá'í asked how much the life of a public officer was worth and what effect the meagerness of this gift would have upon the morals of other men on the police force expected to make that community safe for children.

This resulted in the city council commending the Bahá'í for her activities and service. One member of the council commented:

"It is appropriate that this recognition is given during Brotherhood Week."

What is more interesting is that during the entire drive for funds no mention was made of race—only of the deceased's police activities! And remember—he was *not* a Bahá'í!

Bahá'í groups of four surrounding cities in Pennsylvania opened a special teaching campaign in 1965 to bring the Faith to another city nearby, hoping to acquaint over a thousand families there with the name "Bahá," to invite them to a public gathering and fireside and to let them know that a Bahá'í group would be formed in their town in the near future.

At least five hundred invitations were sent to clubs and professional people, another five hundred fliers were mailed to names listed in the city directory, but a concentrated effort was put on about a thousand house calls in the lower income neighborhoods. At first, a folder was left at the doorways by the Bahá'í children and their friends, announcing the arrival in a few days of other Bahá'ís who would stop to give literature and an important invitation, making it clear that no literature would be sold and no collection taken.

Next, a few days later four teams of two Bahá'ís each began visiting these neighborhoods. Prayer and consultation among the teams preceded each evening of visits. The visitors learned much about this direct approach through experience and the majority of those visited received the Bahá'ís with warmth and courtesy, inviting them in for further conversation.

The meeting subject was "The Time Is Now." It was publicized with paid ads in newspapers, spot radio announcements, and an interview on the local television station. Instead of a number of chairs and a platform for the speaker, the setting of the meeting was made friendly and informal by the arrangement of tables, each table seating nine people, yet all had a good view of the speaker. Each table also had a Bahá'í host to answer questions, and groups were mixed racially.

Over ninety people attended the meeting, at least fifty of whom had never before attended a Bahá'í meeting. The spirit was so warm, friendly, and informal that most guests lingered afterward. The visiting teams continued their work during the following weeks, with further follow-up public meetings, proving a new approach with a lack of motive to force ideas on others could be a means of winning many souls from varied cultural and ethnic groups to the Faith.

One September Sunday evening in Baltimore, Maryland, in the midst of a heavy rainstorm, about one thousand people gathered in a theater for an interracial meeting and special program arranged by the Bahá'ís. Only two of the four speakers were Bahá'ís, but the effect was one of powerful identification with the Faith and its principle, "The Oneness of Mankind." The audience was mixed, with a slight Negro majority.

The main Bahá'í speaker was a Hand of the Cause, and one non-Bahá'í speaker was Lerone Bennett, Jr., well-known Negro writer and Senior Editor of *Ebony* magazine. Mr. Bennett's talk was most significant coming as it did from someone not of the Faith. He prefaced it with a moving tribute to the Birmingham children who had been murdered, and then to the Bahá'í Faith, quoting from Bahá'í writings which emphasize the Bahá'í attitude of racial harmony.

He spoke of the challenge of the Negro struggle to the generally complacent religious community of America and many times he stated how the Bahá'í Faith differs from all other religions in its unswerving efforts to establish racial agreement and eliminate prejudice. He proved his sincerity again many months later when he wrote a long, definitive text on the Faith for *Ebony,* which that magazine published with photos.

Mr. Bennett declared in his talk: "The time for the Negro is now. The dominant drama of this age is the Negro drama—the dominant dream is a Negro dream. But the dream is not of nor for Negroes alone. The dream is as old as Confucius, as wise as Buddha, as gentle as Jesus, as universal as Bahá'u'lláh. . . ."

When the Hand of the Cause came quietly to the microphone he slowly unfolded the dramatic story of a century that has brought mankind the pattern for peace. With ease and compassion he offered the audience the key to understand today's suffering and promise. Quoting from Bahá'u'lláh's letters to the kings, he built up a picture of justice that protects all. Recalling the prophecies of past religions about the flowering of Mount Carmel, he described the beauty of this ancient holy site when it witnessed the election of the first Universal House of Justice.

He proceeded to the potentialities latent in this age and the ability of each individual to recognize the Word of God and to unite with a world-wide Faith destined to heal the ills of humanity. He then carried the audience, completely intent on his words, to a glimpse of tomorrow's world where "every stranger will find a friend, and every enemy a true brother," concluding with the passage from the Bahá'í Writings that states:

"The vitality of men's belief in God is dying out in every land; nothing short of His wholesome medicine can ever restore it."

Besides the many friends the Faith made during this one episode, the young man who snapped the photographs for the later *Ebony* story soon became a Bahá'í, himself!

One of the unique teaching campaigns inaugurated by the Bahá'ís was started in California in September, 1965, when the believers there decided to treat their state as though it were a foreign country, using all kinds of ideas and materials to "invade" the various townships and cities of California in order to strengthen their numbers.

On the first night of this "Victory Campaign," as it was called, over five hundred fireside meetings were held throughout California. Within a month, new declarations came in, new life was poured into Bahá'í communities by the many teaching ideas and meetings for the public, and the imagination and competitive instinct of Bahá'í communities in other parts of the United States flared up into action.

Soon, other "victory" briefings and meetings took place across the country; pioneers went from American areas that had already met their teaching goals to places outside the States that needed help.

A number of successful youth campaigns also took place, and the renewed activities of the American believers were further stimulated by cablegrams of encouragement and approval from the Hands in the Holy Land, those in the Western Hemisphere, and the members of the Universal House of Justice.

Publicity started exploding throughout the United States. CBS-TV showed a *Lamp Unto My Feet* program that included films taken at the World Center and the Wilmette National Headquarters during a Bahá'í Convention. The NBC-TV *Today* Show featured the Faith in a long interview segment. ABC-Radio Network carried a half-hour program. Magazines and newspapers set stories in motion, and the name Bahá'í was no longer something strange and foreign to many Americans preciously unacquainted with it.

The Universal House of Justice's new goals of membership have been constantly met by the various National and Local Assemblies throughout the Bahá'í World, and by 1966, there were already over 25,000 Bahá'í Centers throughout the world, 2,000 of which were in the United States, alone. Mass conversion to the Faith was taking effect in such areas as Venezuela, Korea, Philippines, Burma, Malaysia, Viet-Nam, Thailand, Africa and other countries. News of these and their own victories kept spurring on the American believers to new teaching efforts, since they were also reminded and inspired through the words of their late Guardian that "Victories unsuspected are within reach of the American Bahá'í Community . . . the prize destined for the valiant conquerors are inestimably precious. . . ."

Teaching plans for Bahá'ís pioneering outside their home

town or city have been concentrated either on their settling in the new area or going there for week-end visits to speak or set up public talks by other Bahá'í teachers. Pioneers who are physically, spiritually, and otherwise able to travel, but lack the necessary funds are helped by various national and international funds set up and contributed to by other believers for that purpose, but primarily they are meant to be self-supporting and to secure jobs wherever they settle, so that they can make contacts in their new community as representative members of the civic community.

When a Bahá'í visits or moves to a foreign country that forbids open proselytizing of a religious nature, he is to obey its civil law, but if there is nothing that forbids his having his own Bahá'í books, pictures, and other materials in his new home, he makes certain they are displayed. Should any of his new friends who visit there ask questions about these items, out of politeness a host is required to answer. In this way the Bahá'í Message is often given "subliminally" in areas where active teaching is not allowed.

In the United States, even more than in other countries, the Bahá'í Faith is becoming more of a "youth" movement in both spirit and fact, spontaneously recreating those stirring days of the Dawnbreakers of a century ago. Young people are permitted to affiliate officially with the Faith at the age of fifteen years, and become voting members at the age of twenty-one, but are still considered "youth" until approximately the age of twenty-five. They are the vanguard of the Bahá'í standard-bearers for today, and training to become the pioneers for tomorrow.

In a recent report about the Bahá'í youth projects in America, one sees the firm foundation of belief, sacrifice, and accomplishment already demonstrated by many of these young people who one summer brought to some fifty Bahá'í communities on the continent of North America such magnificent results in example, sacrifice, and teaching of the Faith.

Many Bahá'í concepts are implicit in these youth projects. First and strongest, of course, is obedience to Bahá'u'lláh's admonition to teach the Cause of God; then, reaching the racial minorities in that crucial corollary goal emphasized by Shoghi Effendi. For the youth, teaching and reaching others for the Faith is achieved by teamwork, more than individual effort. Another way in which they accomplish this is by their joyous singing of Bahá'í songs, which so captivates the hearts of those listening that they cannot resist joining in with the rhythm even when they do not know the words.

This has been proven over and over again. One young team of three sang songs on buses, boats, trains, and airlines going between Canada and the United States one summer, and made far greater impact than if they had stood on street corners soapboxing the Bahá'í Message.

To see youth-motivated evenings to which townspeople are invited in areas near summer schools is to watch suspicious strangers become warm friends of the Faith, even when they may not actually become Bahá'ís. Invariably a youth evening to which non-Bahá'ís are invited closes with a Bahá'í song-fest, and the arms of all present, Bahá'ís and invited guests are linked as they sway back and forth to the rhythm of original Bahá'í words and music such as "Passing Through," "Rejoice, Rejoice," "Got Some Teaching to Do," "Who Has Heard of Bahá'u'lláh?" and others.

The two most popular, since they are in fast rhythm, are "Got Some Teaching to Do" and "Who Has Heard of Bahá'u'lláh," written by believers, of course:

Got Some Teaching to Do

(Verse)   You can't change the world with the words of your
          mouth
          You have to live the life in the north and south
          Live the life the whole day through
          O Lord, I've Got Some Teaching To Do!

(Chorus) O Lord, I've Got Some Teaching To Do!
          Don't you call me, Lord, too soon!

(Additional Verses)

> Got to live the life in the East and West
> So the world will see that the Faith is best
> Got to let them know the Faith is true
> O Lord, I've Got Some Teaching To Do!

> Live it in the swamps where the birch trees grow
> Live it in the hills and valleys down below
> Live it with the Christian, Muslim, and Jew
> O Lord, I've Got Some Teaching To Do!

> Live it in the valleys where the tall grass grows
> Live it in the jungle where the elephant goes
> Live it right and live it true
> O Lord, I've Got Some Teaching To Do!

> Live it by the waterfall with its misty shroud
> Live it in the farmlands that the hand of man has
>   plowed
> The masses are waiting the day and night through
> O Lord, I've Got Some Teaching To Do!

Who Has Heard of Bahá'u'lláh?

(Verse)   Long ago the people of all religions
Looked for the Promised One to come
Fulfilling all prophecy that all of humanity
Would some day learn to worship as one.

(Chorus)   Who has heard of Bahá'u'lláh? (3 times)
I've heard the Glad Tidings and I will tell you of
Bahá'u'lláh.

(Verse)   The Báb announced to the people of Persia in
eighteen-forty-four
That He was the Gate through which the Promised
One would come
To unite all from shore to shore.

The Báb was martyred yet His followers grew
And spread the news both far and wide
Among His believers was Husayn 'Alí Who later
for this Cause did die.

(*Chorus*) For that man was Bahá'u'lláh (3 times)
I've heard the Glad tidings and I will tell you of
Bahá'u'lláh

(*Verse*) Husayn 'Alí announced His mission in the year of
eighteen sixty-three
That He was the Promised One sent forth to
humanity
To unite ones like you and me.

His word went forth in the form of Tablets
Which were written in Prison—for you see
Bahá'u'lláh was banished from prison to prison
Just because He wanted all to be free.

Now there are believers in every state
In every country, on islands and seas
United in religion, as was prophesied
This is Bahá'u'lláh's potency.

(*Chorus*)

Now you've heard of Bahá'u'lláh (3 times)
Go spread the Glad Tidings so all may know of
Bahá'u'lláh. . . .

The Bahá'ís realize that the needs of the youth of America
fall within the scope of the Faith. They are spurred on, not de-
terred, by the realization that within a short time 50 percent of
the population of the United States will be young people under
the age of twenty-five.

They also realize that only by adult example within the Faith,
just as in their activities outside of the Faith, can the Bahá'í
youth continue to lead the way for others.

One Candle, Lighting the Darkness

IT IS PROBABLY an easy way out, most people feel, for a writer
to generalize and point out group instances here and there of
Bahá'í sacrifice and endeavor, but occasionally more detail is not
only required but expected.

The only way in which anyone can learn how to progress in anything is through a teacher or an example. The American Bahá'ís, in fact Bahá'ís all over the world, have had many such examples to draw upon in their Bahá'í books and publications, but those in the United States consider themselves most fortunate to exist in a decade that has included in the Faith the living, breathing example of their "Mr. B," as he will be called here(since he refuses to permit personal publicity about himself, and therefore this is the only way in which he can be written about. In fact, until this book appears, he will not even know that this liberty has been taken, and we humbly apologize with the explanation that unless his story is told as symbolical of the great efforts made in the Faith by not only himself but thousands, even hundreds of thousands of believers throughout the universe yesterday, today—even tomorrow—this Faith could not have grown so quickly, so decisively in such a comparatively short time.

Mr. B. is an American who first heard of the Bahá'í Faith in 1940. Until that time his main concern had been his pyramiding radio and television career, along with having to take care of two small sons because of the death of their beloved mother. In the early 1950s he decided to take a puppet animal and create a television show which had him as the only human working with a number of puppet animals.

"It was really the story of my own life," he explained. "An old man when he was young, with a crew haircut and an advertising career, rushing so fast that he was passing up more than he saw. He decided finally to chuck the briefcase and do the things he wanted. By learning to talk to animals he developed a greater understanding of people. As I thought of that, I felt that something had to be changed in my own life!"

What he didn't realize at the moment was that the "something" had already changed his life when he met Miss M., the young lady who was to become his second wife, who introduced the Faith to him during an interview with her on one of his own radio programs. After they married, when she took on the care of his two sons, she encouraged and agreed with all his efforts for the Faith. Therefore, when he felt he wanted to change his life, after prayer and consultation with Mrs. M. and the two boys, they knew it didn't matter that he would be giving up more money than he had ever earned before in his life, and the career he had previously wanted.

He still grins when he thinks about it. "In those days everything was so wonderful financially there wasn't even time to go to the bank. When the call first came for pioneers I was sure annoyed at everyone *else* for not going! Finally I got the idea. The call wasn't just for everyone else—it was also for *me!* I had a contract with this seven-year thing where you can't breathe because of sponsors looking down your neck," a contract, incidentally, which he never admits he spent twenty years working hard to achieve, "and we couldn't seem to get out of it. So??? We just prayed and prayed. And what do you think? The sponsor had a strike, the factory closed down temporarily, and they came and *begged* me to release *them,* and I said very loudly, very happily, 'You're released!' Just another of those wonderful Bahá'í happenings. . . ."

As far as Mr. B. and Mrs. M. are concerned, everything that's happened since is still "wonderful." They discount with a shrug that they plunged from a life of what had been definite financial prosperity to one that was to be in the future "mildly rocky," to say the least. Sometimes it took a great deal of laughter—for which they thank Bahá'u'lláh since He gave them both a marvelous sense of humor amid the worst sort of disasters—along with prayer, to keep them going.

For instance. They thought they had enough money to last ten years when they decided to pioneer in Africa, as their first step. Instead, their funds vanished within two years! Partly because they realized that bank accounts cannot stretch when the meal to which they've invited four invited guests has to be enlarged to include a houseful, as it often did in Africa.

They also bought a large farm on the outskirts of a big African city, which they were certain would make money, because of the hundreds of fruit trees there. As they put it, when spring arrived, there was a great crop of new Bahá'ís but little fruit on the trees because they had been too busy teaching the Faith to spray the trees.

The one farm crop with which they succeeded—4,500 crowns of asparagus—they learned to regret. How was Mr. B. to know that would be the very year that the import duty would be lowered, making their crop a total money loss? As time went on, if they were invited to other homes, they were also told, "No asparagus, please. . . ."

One pioneer wrote to Mr. B. about his own difficulties, mainly health. He received a long humorous account of what had actually happened to Mr. B. during his years of pioneering abroad. Although it was written tongue-in-cheek, it was actually a *curtailed* list of the many things than can happen to a determined but disaster-prone or test-ridden believer:

> . . . in a part of Africa, where I had tick fever, with accompanying high fevers, I remember the delightful day when M. went shopping, while I was supposed to nap. The African boy woke me up shoting *"Noka, Noka,"* which means "snake." so I staggered out with my .22 rifle and shot a cobra. A few minutes after I returned to bed, there were loud cries of another snake. This time my high temperature caused me to have double vision and, like the old Irish joke, I saw not one, but three, waving hoods open. I remembered what my father always said, "When in doubt, shoot the one in the middle." I did—and missed. Fortunately it slunk away, frightened by the noise. . . .
>
> On the way back to bed I stepped on a broken bottle and was too knocked out to do more than wrap a bath towel around it to stop the bleeding and throw myself on the bed. I flung out a hand—and a spider bit my thumb! And just then, in walked my beautiful wife, beaming happily from her excursion.
>
> "What kind of day did you have, dear?" she asked with wifely enthusiasm.
>
> "I'm in a losing streak," was all I could say.

He then concluding this encouraging recital with: "And after hepatitis, there was the son of hepatitis, every spring. In rapid succession, I also had Asiatic flu, pneumonia, a torn ligament and a few angina heart attacks. Otherwise, nothing really bad to write of. . . ."

His correspondent quickly cabled: I GET THE MESSAGE, B. NEVER FELT BETTER IN MY LIFE.

One time this pioneering family was down to exactly $3.15 and Mr. B. took on a writing-announcing-producing job at an African radio station. It was a coast-to-coast program, from the Indian Ocean to the Atlantic. In between recording a stack of programs, Mr. B taught the Faith in surrounding areas. He received per week from this "network" show the equivalent to what he had been paid for a five-minute spot in the States, but all he wanted was eating, traveling, and teaching money for himself and family, so he didn't mind.

He found that as more and more Bahá'ís followed his example by pioneering to Africa and helping with the teaching work there, it changed the response of the Africans to the white people. They saw in the believers such love, warmth, and appreciation for themselves that they came to accept and appreciate the Bahá'í attitude about equality of all kinds.

When the Bahá'í Temple was dedicated at Kampala, Uganda, Africa, this attitude of oneness of mankind was demonstrated in the number of African believers, newly enrolled in the Faith, who came from formerly warring tribes and gathered there in such love and warmth and harmony.

At the time Mr. B. was recovering from another of his physical catastrophes about which he always makes so light. He often held meetings from his bed, and noticed an African refusing to enter the room with the others. Mr. B. pretended not to see him and continued his discussion with the other guests. Slowly the reluctant one sidled over and gradually progressed until he was sitting on the bed. He remained there, obviously smiling and happy, patting his host's hand from time to time. Suddenly he drew back and stared at the hand he was holding. In awe he remarked: "Do you know something? You not as *white* as you used to be!"

Mr. B. has written many books, radio programs, and other materials on the Faith. Since dedicating his main part of his life to working for the Faith, after five years in Africa, he was appointed a Hand of the Cause and during the next five years spent half his time in Haifa and the other half traveling and teaching throughout Europe, Latin America, Alaska, and Africa. He has probably traveled around the world a dozen times in that period.

Mr. B. is one of the few people who gives his friends a feeling of optimism when they hear he is bedded again.

"Good!" they cry out. "He'll stay put for a while and maybe write another book or think of some marvelous new teaching plan for us!"

But early in 1964 they weren't feeling so optimistic. Throughout the Bahá'í world there was only grief at the news their beloved Mr. B. had suffered still another angina attack. He was returned to the United States, California, to convalesce, but this time there was prayer, and very little hope.

To everyone's surprise, once again he got up and with his wonderful wife started out teaching and working as hard as ever. The international administrative body tried to help Mr. B. take things easier by assigning him to live for the next few years in the Western Hemisphere. Instead, between having other ailments and physical problems, he has worked just as hard in various parts of America and Canada as he formerly did anywhere else.

When he first became a Bahá'í pioneer, Mr. B. had thick black hair, a black moustache, tall athletic body, firm jawline, sparkling brown eyes, an aquiline nose, and a magnetic voice. The nose is still aquiline, but the hair has thinned, the moustache has grayed, and the waistline has expanded. However, the eyes still sparkle, the voice still propels, and the dedication to the Faith has never wavered.

His wife insists he would probably find something to laugh about under any circumstances, no matter how bad. When they were both very sick one time, lying in an African hut, with rain coming through the roof, malaria burning them up, and Mr. B's infected foot preventing his even hobbling, he could still chuckle when an African boy came in to ask whether they required anything else.

"Certainly," Mr. B. whispered. "A small portion of smallpox!"

Whenever someone remarks that they must have lived on pretty short rations at times, Mr. B.'s eyes twinkle as he looks at his wife, and answers:

"Often we thought we'd be on the streets shouting, 'Cockles and mussels, alive, alive ho!' for something to eat, instead of shouting the Name of Bahá'u'lláh!"

It doesn't take anyone longer than five minutes to fall under the magnetic spell of Mr. B. and his wife. But when he tells of the sacrifices made by innumerable other Bahá'í pioneers, there is no laughter, in fact Mr. B. weeps openly, making one realize that most of his laughter only covers the deep seriousness in his makeup.

The American believers realize that Mr. B.'s health will never be perfect since he ignores doctors' orders by continuing his strenuous Bahá'í schedule the moment any new physical crisis simmers down, and rejoice that in 1966 he and his wife returned to their beloved Africa where their youngest son lives, while the oldest one lives in California and has three small children.

However, all Bahá'ís know that not only the future of Mr. B. and his family, but that of all those who put themselves in Bahá'u'lláh's Hands is not at their own disposal. Whatever comes up for these sacrificing souls is accepted gladly, whether it be to help gain victories for the Faith or to conserve their strength for other Bahá'í endeavors.

That is the path of the true believer. To be as a candle lighting the darkness for others. And the power of many candles shining in the dark can be very great, indeed. . . .

Summation, Personal Comment,
Acknowldegntsme

Summation

THERE it is.

The background, the meaning, the development of the Faith of Bahá'u'lláh.

It needs only a few paragraphs to outline its future plans.

The believers have learned that they have the capacity to accomplish at any time the definitive goals assigned to them, goals through which the Cause has already become established physically, socially, and spiritually throughout the world.

The spark lit by the Báb and Bahá'u'lláh has at last become a conflagration warming the hearts and souls of people the world over.

Coming up is the second election of the Universal House of Justice. Before that, the Centenary of Bahá'u'lláh's Proclamation of His Message to the Kings and Rulers of the World will have been observed, which celebration will have included a program of proclaiming this same Message of Bahá'u'lláh to those in the world today who could not possibly have heard It originally.

There will also have been six Intercontinental Conferences for Bahá'ís, held in Panama City, Chicago, Sydney, Kampala, Frankfurt, and New Delhi, with accompanying details being given to all the communications media throughout the world.

The international scene by 1973 will have seen the completion of the final years of the Nine-Year Plan of the Universal House of Justice. Starting in August 1968 there would have been held such further Bahá'í Oceanic Conferences as had long before been predicted by Shoghi Effendi, starting with one on an island in the Mediterranean Sea, to commemorate Bahá'u'lláh's Voyage upon that Sea a century before, when He traveled from Gallipoli, Turkey, to the Most Great Prison in 'Akká, and followed subsequently with Oceanic Conferences in the Atlantic Ocean, Caribbean Sea, Pacific Ocean, and Indian Ocean.

During all this, the Bahá'ís remember how their beloved Guardian had previously launched his own two international teaching campaigns and that in 1953 there had begun the remarkable World Crusade under his direction. Even to those who are not believers, it should be stimulating to learn of the remarkable progress this Faith has made since the time when Shoghi Effendi called upon the widely scattered Bahá'í World community to embark upon its first large teaching crusade.

Today the Faith of Bahá'u'lláh and its believers cannot be called scattered. Theirs has become one great international community, its members united in dedication to something that is more than a world-embracing ideal.

To observe the lives, the deeds, the accomplishments of the Faith in gathering more and more thinking people under the Bahá'í banner, in bringing meaning to mankind's ideal of oneness, is to be assured that this is no longer just a dream. It is something within reach of all those who truely want it to become a reality!

Personal Comment

THIS POEM has been written by the author for inclusion here:

Awakening

I sat there quietly—alone . . .
Just thanking God
For all the joy He's given me

Of finding Him . . .
My future holds the clearness of a stream
Reflecting life's true goodness
And I know how God so often works
Through some small vessel to renew its faith—
Like me . . .

I sat there thanking God
For every time He's filled me with delight
Until my heart has room for nothing any more
But loving thanks—Compassion—and the sum of
Understanding for His way . . .

I sat there quietly—at last . . .
And felt the healing truth that we are but His ploys—
He never shapes our destinies, but only fits them
To the pattern of His need
A pattern that permits no knowledge of mere
Lust or greed . . .

I sat there weeping for
The ones with sadness in their souls
Who cannot know as I the stillness of this Dawn
When Darkness has escaped the world
To leave the calm assurance of Tomorrow—
Here Today—
Because I am at last in love with Love
And with pure joy
Can pray . . .

Frankly, one of my reasons for weeping was because at last I *had* learned how to pray, because it had taken me, just as it has taken many others, so many years to learn the joy of communication with God.

Please do not judge the contents of this book by the human limitations of its compiler. If there has been any error in transmission of the Ideals and Teachings of the Bahá'í Faith, this could not be helped and was certainly not intended. There are no errors in the Divine Plan, only in the manner in which it is demonstrated, and since Bahá'ís are assured of divine understanding and

acceptance of their human frailties, it is hoped for your understanding and forgiveness of the author's.

I am not a "religious" individual in the sense that many are
accustomed to think in giving that designation to someone who
becomes completely engrossed in the religious life. The Bahá'í
"life" is that of living a completely human existence, but of trying
to improve its quality along the path of search. I suffer for others
in a very rational, normal way, but I suffer more for not always
being able to give to others what I so selfishly seek for myself—
understanding, a love that asks for nothing—not even for love
in return—and the ability to accept others' faults with their
virtues. However, I keep trying, and that is the first step to leading the good life—to want to try and to know you will continue
to try in spite of your failures.

Bahá'ís believe in meditation, but I try not to meditate upon
myself too much, because that would be a sheer waste of the time
given for my use on earth. Of course, this is purely my own personal opinion, but Bahá'ís are supposed to be "individuals," and
the flowers of one "garden" are not alike, either.

In addition, not believing that anything but this manuscript
will have any lasting value in my life, it comforts me to know that
those thoughts and ideas which are truly divine will remain time-
less and important after I am gone.

I joined the Bahá'í Faith in 1938. It was not until 1963 that
I determined to be more than a "believer," to start trying to prove
the validity of those teachings I have always loved. Mine is no
shining example, however, to admit it took so many years to stop
blaming others for my own faults of both omission and commis-
sion. When I threw away the veils of constant self-interest which
clouded my vision, then I knew why life in a Bahá'í World, filled
with association with my Bahá'í "family," was the only real thing
for me. The past is now truly the past, and today I am freer and
oh, so very much happier.

How glad I am to have finally realized how much the Faith
can make use of me—of my obedience, understanding, and, most

of all, my dedication. This eventually does happen, of course, to those who sincerely desire to find meaning to their earthly existence. Today I can wear my beliefs, not as a cloak of goodness with which to impress others, but as a spiritual skin into which I pray some day truly to fit.

As a Bahá'í teacher, I am not permitted to force my beliefs on others, but in various ways I can try to express them. If whatever has been written in these pages enables anyone to appreciate what so many already believe, then he will also appreciate the Bahá'í attitude that he learned of the Bahá'í Faith because he had done something pleasing to God.

I have a wonderful husband, a lovely daughter, a career, and my Faith. I also have many friends in and out of the Faith. As a writer, I may work on other writing projects, but as a Bahá'í I shall do nothing that delights me more than this book, not in the sense of something personally accomplished, but as an offering of belief in and love for Bahá'u'lláh.

This cannot be considered all "my" work. There is very little that is truly original in its contents, except occasional phrasing, at best. As the acknowledgments will state, everything in this book has been culled either from the Bahá'í Writings, Bahá'í teachers, or Bahá'í friends. I have been privileged to know, to meet, to be with and to love so many wonderful believers who have given selflessly of their time and Bahá'í knowledge to me so that our teachings could be shared informally with others. I can only thank them again and again, most humbly and most gratefully, for their contributions to this effort, with the regret that there is not enough space to say how very much I appreciate their patience and forbearance.

There are other writers in or out of the Faith who could have compiled this book far better than I have, but I honestly do not feel they could have done it more gratefully, more humbly aware of the privilege than this author. In putting it together I have been able to restudy the workings of my own soul and to learn once more that for me, anyway, there is nothing else that can equal the excitement of being a Bahá'í.

Externally I may seem no different to those who have known me over the years, but inside myself I know the difference, because as a Bahá'í there is nowhere else for me to go but steadily, albeit slowly, forward.

For anyone whose soul has been stirred by the knowledge that there are these wonderful teachings, it has been my pleasure to acquaint him with the Dawn of a New Day.

Acknowledgments

GRATITUDE is expressed for permission to use copywrited quotations from the books published by the Bahá'í Publishing Trust of the United States, 110 Linden Avenue, Wilmette, Illinois 60091, to which you may address inquiries about these titles. All questions about Bahá'í Centers should be addressed to the National Spiritual Assembly of the Bahá'ís of the United States, 536 Sheridan Road, Wilmette, Illinois 60091.

There were other Bahá'í books and materials used which are not available for general sale and are therefore not listed here.

I wish to acknowledge the invaluable help of the many believers without whose kindness and generosity and knowledge this book could not have been created, either. Some of them gave of their long years of Bahá'í study and research, others corrected misinformation I had, and still others were models of patience and love in giving of their time and cooperation. Some, of course, did not know how much they were contributing from their talks, their tapes, their classes, their writings, and some have left behind reams of material although they themselves have progressed to other "Worlds of God," but they all share equally in the bounties that may result for Bahá'u'lláh from this cooperative effort.

The Bahá'í Faith has many sources of comfort for those who feel lost, lonely or blinded through the events of each day. My own has come from a prayer that was given to the believers by Bahá'u'lláh for just one reason—to turn their hearts and souls to the Source of All Good, All Meaning—at least once a day. It becomes a daily goal not to neglect turning to God—preferably at noon—and with this prayer I achieve surcease from all pain, all doubt and all darkness for at least the few moments it takes to say and meditate about its meaning.

If this book gives nothing else to those who seek a new Answer to what Life is about, perhaps they will accept the Gift of these Words that may bring them closer to God:

Bahá'í Obligatory Noon-Day Prayer

I bear witness, O my God
That Thou hast created me to know Thee
And to worship Thee
I testify at this moment to my powerlessness
And to Thy Might
To my poverty
And to Thy Wealth
There is no other God but Thee
The Help in peril
The Self-sustaining . . .

And to all who read this book, as well as my husband Jack, a non-Bahá'í whose pure soul and loving cooperation made all things possible.—Thank You.

Index

Abbood, House of, 72–73
ABC Radio, 200
'Abdu'l-Bahá, 11, 25, 56, 71*ff*, 77–111*ff*, 162*ff;* bank account, 120; and Christianity, 17; death, last rites of, 102–07; defines Bahá'í, 21; on heaven, the soul, death, 188, 189–90, 191; joyousness in hardship, 186; last will and testament, 107–11, 146–47, 162; love for enemies, 187; and Mary Maxwell, 117; and Negroes (*see* Negroes and racial prejudice); in North America, 17, 89–101, 117, 158–59; permission for Wilmette temple, 168; physical descriptions, 75, 91–92, 118; on politics, 33; on prayer, 185; relics, mementoes, 153*ff;* on smoking, 31; on teaching, 192; work habits, 126–27
'Abdu'lláh Effendi Mukhlis, 106
Abraham, 79, 80
Acre. *See* 'Akká (Acre)
Administrative Order, 19–27*ff*, 108–10. *See also specific bodies*
Adrianople, 67–70, 153
Africa, 12, 15, 147, 206–10; Kampala, Uganda, 17, 208; Kitali Prison, 128
Ahmad-Ahsá'í, 49
'Akká (Acre), 70–76, 85, 86, 87, 105, 111, 168
Alcoholic beverages, 30–31, 35
Allenby, Edmund Henry Hynman

Allenby, 1st Viscount, 104, 106, 160
America. *See* North America; United States and Americans
Archives. *See* International Archives
Art, 40
Assemblies, 108, 167. *See also* Local Spiritual Assemblies; National Assemblies
Auxiliary Boards, 142*ff*
Awakening (poem), 212–13

"B., Mr.," 205–10
Báb, the, 11–12, 25, 48–56*ff*, 85, 146; and calendar, 36; and the Covenant, 80; precious sites purchased, 116; relics in archives, 153, 154; tomb on Mt. Carmel; Shrine of, 17, 56, 88, 106, 113, 121, 129, 143
Baghdád, 59–65, 66, 157
Bahá'í News, 178
Bahá'u'lláh, 8–9*ff*, 21*ff*, 56–76, 82*ff*, 113; and building of temples, 169; celebration of voyage, 212; centenary of proclamation, 211; Covenant, 77–82; and divorce, 29; and Hands of the Cause, 142; and House of Justice, 146, 147; and justice, 45; and last will of 'Abdu'l-Bahá, 107*ff*; and money, 120; on moral code; 41–42; and number nine, 37; and politics, 33, 170; precious sites pur-

chased, 116; relics, mementoes in archives, 153–54, 154–55, 156–57; resemblance to, of Shoghi Effendi, 118; and soul; hereafter, 188–89, 190–91; and teaching, 191, 193
Bahjí, 74–76, 86, 113, 114, 120, 131; Mrs. Hearst's picture at, 90
Baltimore, Md., 198–99
Bennett, Lerone, Jr., 198–99
Berkeley, Calif., 95
Black Hole, the, 57–59, 116
Blomfeld, Lady, 102
Bourgeois, Louis, 173–75
Brahma, 83
British government, 102, 104, 160
Browne, Edward G., 75
Buddha and Buddhism, 10, 83
Burial. See Funerals
Búshihr, 116
Buyuk Khanum, 159

Caiaphas, Rabbi, 84
Calendar, 35–37
California, 199–200. See also specific cities
Canada, 89, 110, 117, 133, 162, 169
Caribbean area, 172
CBS-TV, 200
Cedric, S.S., 91
Central America, 110
Chicago, Ill., 168, 169, 179. See also Willmette, Ill., temple and properties
Chinese, the, 82
Christianity. See Jesus Christ and Christianity
Churchill, Winston, 160
Cleanliness, 63

Collins, Mrs. Amelia, 137
Columbian Exposition, 168
Committees, 44, 172
Community, 22–27ff
Constantinople, 65–67, 69, 87, 88, 116
Contributions. See Funds
Covenant, 77–82

Dahlberg, Dr. Edwin T., 7–8
Death, 187–91 (see also Funerals); obligation to leave written will and testament, 35, 38
Decision-making, 26–27
Divorce, 27, 29–30

Ebony magazine, 198–99
Education, 10, 17, 42 (see also Schools; Teaching); Green Acre School, 96–98
Eliot, Me., 96–98
European Teaching Project, 110

Farmer, Sarah, 97
Fasting, 35, 36–37
Ferraby, John, 140
"Firesides," 21
Frankfurt, Germany, 17
Funds (contributions), 35, 39–40, 171, 176
Funerals, 35, 42; 'Abdu'l-Bahá's, 105–06; Shoghi Effendi's, 136–40

Gabriel, Angel, 57
Gambling, 30, 35
Gardens, 114, 120, 130, 131, 177–78; Ridvan, 65, 66, 73, 76
Germany, 170; Frankfurt, 17; Hitler, 10

Getsinger, Lua, 100
Gilbert, Rabbi Arthur, 170
God, 9–10, 27, 41, 49, 79. *See also specific prophets*
God Passes By, 116
"Got Some Teaching to Do," 202–03
Government, 31–34
Great Britain. *See* British government; London
Greatest Holy Leaf, The, 105, 114, 125; and relics, 153, 154–55, 156, 159–60
Green Acre School, 96–98
Gregorian Calendar, 36
Gregory, Louis, 94
Groups, 22, 193

Haifa, 12, 88, 101–07, 113–14, 119–22*ff* (*see also specific Holy Places;* international Bahá'í bodies); archives in, 151–61
Haiti, 12
Hands of the Cause of God, 25, 142–45, 149*ff*, 198*ff*; and Shoghi Effendi's death, funeral, 135*ff*
Hearst, Mrs. Phoebe, 90, 168
Heaven, 188
Hell, 188
Hitler, Adolf, 10
Holidays (Holy Days), 36–38, 42, 171
Holy Places, 120–21, 143. *See also* Haifa; *specific places*
Home for the Aged, 178
Hospitality, 21
Houses of Worship, 17. *See also specific places*
Humility, 185–87

Husayn 'Alí. *See* Bahá'u'lláh

Illinois, 194–96. *See also* specific cities
India, 12
Integration. *See* Negroes and racial prejudice
Intercalary Days, 36
International Archives, 114, 130, 132, 151–61
International Bahá'í Council, 115, 143, 145
International Conferences, 211
International Headquarters. *See* Haifa
Iran. *See* Persia
Islám, 11, 113 (*see also* Muhammad; Muhammadans); Shi'ih sect, 54
Israel (*see also* Haifa; Palestine): government of, 138–39, 143
Istanbul. *See* Constantinople

Japanese Young Men's Christian Association, 95
Jesus Christ and Christianity, 10–11, 13, 48, 54, 55, 70; and covenant, 79, 80; and dove, 57; and education, 16–17; and love, 83
Jews and Judaism, 11, 13 (*see also* Israel; Moses); Hebrew Calendar, 36
Judaism. *See* Jews and Judaism
Julian Calendar, 36
Justice, 45–46. *See also* Universal House of Justice

Kampala, Uganda, Africa, 17, 208
Kitali Prison, 128

Lamp Unto My Feet (TV program), 200
Lao-tze, 82
Laws, ordinances, obligations, 27–43*ff*. *See also* Covenant; Universal House of Justice
Letters of the Living, 51, 52–53, 154
Literature, 40
Local Spiritual Assemblies, 22–24*ff*, 43–47, 108, 115, 167, 193
London, 130–42; World Congress, 15, 117, 149
Love, 182–85

Mah-kú, 116
Marriage(s), 27–30, 40, 42, 114, 171; Shoghi Effendi's, 124–25; at Wilmette temple, 180
Mary the Magdalen, 84
Masons, 31
Material possessions, 42. *See also* Money
Maxwell, Mary. *See* Ruhiyyih Khanum
Maxwell, Sutherland and May Bolles, 89, 117, 128
Maxwell Home, 100
Mayberry, Mrs. Florence, 129–30
Mazra'ih, 74, 86, 114
Military service, 34–35
Money, 120. *See also* Funds
Morals, 40–43, 44–45
Moses, 13, 16, 55, 83; and covenant, 79, 80
Mount Carmel, 74, 106, 114, 131, 132. *See also* Haifa; *specific Holy Places, etc.*
Mount Salvat, 96
Muhammad, 13, 16, 55, 57, 83; and Covenant, 80–81; descendants entitled to wear green, 52, 138
Muhammadans (Muslims) (*see also* Islám; Muhammad): Calendar of, 36; Persian, 49
Muhlschlegel, Dr. Adelbert, 137
Mullá Husayn, 49–51, 52
Music, 180–81; songs, 202–04
Muslims. *See* Muhammadans (Muslims)

Narcotics, 30, 31, 35
National Assemblies, 44–45, 108, 110, 115, 147, 167. *See also* specific countries
NBC-TV, 200
Negroes and racial prejudice, 12, 90–91, 93–94, 170, 194–99
New Year, 36, 37
New York City, 15, 91, 94, 99, 100–01, 158–59
Nine, the number, 13, 175
Nine-Year Plan, 212
Nineteen-Day Feasts, 35–38, 39, 44, 187
Noon-Day Prayer, 217
North America, 89–101, 110, 162–81. *See also* United States
Nudism, 40
Numbers "9," "19," 37, 175

Obedience, 183–84
Obligations. *See* Laws, ordinances, obligations
Oceanic Conferences, 212
Ordinances. *See* Laws, ordinances, obligations
Ottoman government and the Turks, 65–67*ff*, 84, 87, 88, 107–08

Palestine, 101–03ff, See also Israel; specific places
Palo Alto, Calif., 95
Parsees, 83
Peary, Adm. Robert, 93
Pennsylvania, 197
Persia(ns) (Iran), 17, 48–50ff, 116, 156
Peter, St., 80, 84
Pioneers, 39, 88–89, 115, 117, 192–94ff
Politics, 31–34, 35, 170
Prejudice, 10, 12. See also Negroes and racial prejudice
Prophets, 7–8ff. See also specific prophets
Publicity, 200
Publishing Trust, 172, 178, 179
Purest Branch, the, 71, 72, 158

Quddús, 53

Racial prejudice. See Negroes and racial prejudice
Registration cards, 24–25
Riḍván Festival, 65
Riḍván Gardens, 65, 66; named by 'Abdu'l-Bahá, 73, 76
Root, Martha, 122
Ruhiyyih Khanum (Mary Maxwell), 103, 117–42, 143; and completing of archives, 151–52, 155–56, 157

Sám Khán, 55–56
San Francisco, Calif., 94–95
Schools (see also Education): and Holy Days, 171
Seven-Year Plan, 115ff, 176
Sexual relations, 30, 40
Shi'ih sect, 54

Shíráz, 154
Shoghi Effendi Rabbani (the Guardian), 9, 20, 53ff, 76, 105ff, 111–42ff; on 'Abdu'l-Bahá's death, 102–03; on 'Abdu'l-Bahá's U.S. visit, 98–99; and archives building, relics, 152, 160; and binoculars, 158; illness, death of; last rites, 130–42; on Letters of the Living, 53; on Nineteen-Day Feast, 38; on politics, 31–33; and separation of Canada and the U.S.; growth of U.S. assembly, 162, 164ff, 200; and teaching, 176, 192; wedding of, 124–25; work habits of, 125–26
Shrine of the Báb. See under Báb, the
Síyáh-Chál, 57–59, 85, 116
Siyyid Kázim, 49
Smoking, 31
Songs, 202–04
Soul, the, 187–91
South America, 110
Stanford University, 95
Supreme Legislative Body. See Universal House of Justice
Sydney, Australia, 17

Táhirh, 53, 85
Tákur, 116
Teaching, 35, 110, 191–210. See also Education; Pioneers
Ten-Year Crusade, 148, 149
Thompson, Juliet, 100
Ṭihrán, 85, 111
Tobin, Nettie, 100
Today (TV show), 200
Turkestan, 173

Turkey. *See* Ottoman government and the Turks; *specific cities*

Turner, Mr. (butler), 90

United States and Americans, 89–101, 110, 133, 158–59, 162–81 (*see also specific individuals, places*); and funerals, 42; and Holy Days, 42, 171; marriage, divorce in, 27, 42, 171; and politics, 31, 32; military service, 34

Universal House of Justice, 25–26, 145–51, 199, 200, 211; 'Abdu'l-Bahá plans, 108, 110, 146–47; and archives, 161; International Bahá'í Council a forerunner of, 115, 143, 145; Nine-Year Plan of, 212

Utah, 196–97

Viet-Nam, 10, 12

Voting, 32, 33

Washington, D.C., 92–93

Weddings. *See* Marriage(s)

"Who Has Heard of Bahá'u'-lláh?," 203–04

Will and testament, last, 35–38. *See also* specific wills

Wilmette, Ill., temple and properties, 17, 100, 110, 116, 153, 166–81, 192; films of, on TV, 200

World Center. *See* Haifa

World Crusade, 110. *See also* Shoghi Effendi

World Order magazine, 178

World War I, 101

World War II, 176–77

Work, 185–86. *See also* Teaching; *specific people*

Worship, work, and humility, 185–87

Year of Patience, 29–30

Youth, 200, 201–04

Zoroaster, 57, 83